# Practical Current Awareness Services From Libraries

# Practical Current Awareness Services From Libraries

Edited by
Tom Whitehall

Gower

Published by
Gower Publishing Company Limited
Gower House, Croft Road
Aldershot
Hants GU11 3HR
England

Gower Publishing Company
Old Post Road
Brookfield
Vermont 05036
USA

**British Library Cataloguing in Publication Data**

Practical current awareness services from
libraries.
1.  Current awareness services
I.   Whitehall, T.
025.5'25          Z674.4

**Library of Congress Cataloging-in-Publication Data**

Practical current awareness services from libraries.
    Bibliography: p.
    Includes index.
    1. Current awareness services.  2. Reference services
    (Libraries) 3. Library science – Data processing.
I. Whitehall, T.
Z764.4.P73 1986     025.5     86-9889

Printed in Great Britain at the University Press, Cambridge.

ISBN 0  566  03519  7

# Contents

# List of contributors

*Alan Blick*, Beecham Pharmaceuticals, Research Division
*Richard Golland*, GLC Research Library
*Philip Hathaway*, GLC Methodology Group
*Jane Rogers*, J. P. Kenny and Partners
*C. J. Want*, STC Technology Ltd
*Tom Whitehall*, Loughborough University of Technology

# Preface

This book is about the attempt by information workers in industry and government to help and encourage professionals to make use of new information on their work and interests. Of course, this does not mean that it will not be useful to academic librarians or information workers in the public sector — in fact, one of the benefit studies reported was made among the clients of an academic library. The phrase 'from libraries' is included in the title to indicate that the main focus of the book is on the management of current awareness service based on a collection of documents made deliberately to cater for the requirements for information of a group of professional people. That this may not be the way of the future is one of the threads that runs through the book.

In 1947 Fleming, a university librarian, provided his clients with a 'continuous bibliographic service' by laying out for their attention items of recently acquired literature, and notifying that reader of their availability. These items were selected on the basis of Fleming's knowledge of the reader's interests. Current awareness service from libraries is now approaching middle age, and seems at the moment to be going through a bad time.

The golden age of current awareness service was most probably the early 1960s. At that time the larger companies began to hire chemists, engineers and biologists to work in or alongside their libraries, or they transferred staff from the laboratory, in order to have people who could read the vast amount of technical literature and recognise ideas of value to the research and development effort. At bottom there was the assumption that an information service has value to professional people. But in these libraries more was at stake — the documentation of the organisation's own experience in the technical area, and the development of systems to be used in the future to ensure the profitable exploitation of information from inside and outside the company. The information workers of that time gave a current awareness service, and made retrospective searches for their clients, but they also developed systems for handling internal and external information. The newly available computers, and news from America of how they could be used for documentation purposes, gave a spur to these efforts. The job of in-house information worker evolved in another direction as well. In the 1970s it was possible to see 'information analysts' working in government and industrial libraries. These are subject specialists who compile digests and reviews of new information for middle and upper management.

The benefit to the client from a current awareness service is threefold. It keeps the client in touch with what is going on — generally, in the area of his organisation's interest, and specifically, on topics of importance to the client. It can thus supply useful methods, ideas, concepts, experience or information which can result in a saving of project time, can inform a client's ideas on a topic, or can give ideas for new work. Those workers who are in the habit of keeping themselves up to date can use a current awareness service to save time they might otherwise spend in looking through current publications for items of possible interest. *But mainly a current awareness service has value in that it does something for professional workers which they may never do for themselves – either because they are unconvinced of the value of keeping up to date, or because, even though they know its value, they can make no time available to look at published material.*

Unfortunately the benefits from current awareness service are less obvious to the casual observer that its cost. One of the chief pressures on current awareness service from libraries arises from the labour-intensive nature of the traditional service. The labour cost of a service which involves subject specialists spending up to a third of their time in scanning the literature forms a substantial part of its total cost. This means that in order to continue a current awareness service based on scanning, the information manager must be able to maintain a sufficiently adequate staff. At a time when cost-efficiency is so important to senior management, this is very difficult.

Since the middle 1960s it has been possible to buy sets of references produced from searching computerised abstracting and indexing services, and this fact presents another threat to the traditional current awareness service, because expenditure on materials from outside is often more readily agreed by one's manager than expenditure on staff. Larger organisations were able to lease the tapes from a and i service producers, and search them on their own computers to give a centralised service of notifications to staff in many departments, thus reducing the need to maintain local scanning effort.

More recently the ready availability of communication links and the acquisition by professionals of computer terminals at their workplace has added a third threat to in-house scanning of the literature as the basis for current awareness service – that it appears to duplicate what a professional worker can easily do for himself by a subject search through an on-line database!

These pressures, and the necessity to choose between many alternative approaches to current awareness service, once the decision to give a service has been made, present serious problems for today's information manager.

By presenting a variety of material this book attempts to illuminate some of these problems. The book is not a recipe of ready-made solutions as much as a record of ways of doing and thinking about current awareness service from which the reader can benefit through his or her own actions. In particular, approaches to service are more often discussed in terms of their effectiveness than their cost-efficiency, and it is shown how benefits to the clients of current awareness services can be demonstrated.

Chapter 1 describes alternative approaches to current awareness service. In Chapter 2 a method for choice between alternatives is described which does more than compare their cost. Chapters 3 to 5 describe several different approaches to the problem of the high labour cost of current awareness — co-operative scanning arrangements, computerised compilation, and the use of input from secondary bibliographic services to supplement in-house scanning. Chapter 6 reports the results of a recent review of how industrial information units have reacted to the pressures on current awareness service. The book concludes with a chapter on techniques for demonstrating benefit to the clients of a current awareness service, and for evaluating effectiveness. These are illustrated by examples of recent evaluations.

If you believe in the classical aim of current awareness service — that it supplies professional people with something they might never obtain for themselves — then this book is for you.

# 1        Alternatives for current awareness service (CAS)

*Tom Whitehall*

### Aims for effective CAS

An ideal current awareness service for professional workers would look something like this:

> Subject specialists, working alongside their clients, would scan current literature of all kinds, and look out for items which contributed in some way to their work. When they found them they would notify clients individually by supplying at first an indication of just what it was that was potentially useful, and why.

This ideal conception of CAS seldom happens in real life. For one thing, information workers rarely get close enough to their clients. There are often not enough information workers available to offer such personal service, and there are problems of confidence and delegation to overcome before such an arrangement can be made to work. For another thing, much useful current awareness service is given by people who are not subject experts in any area.

However, knowledge of a client's interests is a basic requirement for CAS and there are other requirements which, if satisfied, lead to a service which can provide useful material and is easy to use.

*Coverage* It goes without saying that the subject coverage of input to a current awareness service should be appropriate. A knowledge of sources is important here, as well as a knowledge of clients' work and interests. Coverage of different types of source is equally important, because the success of professional work can rest on a complete knowledge of patents or standards or legislation on a critical topic.

*Timeliness* In some cases the elapsed time between publication of new material and notification of it to a client is important. News of competitive activities, products and projects, news of new materials or processes are examples of this. Here the sources that are scanned should include ones that contain up-to-the-minute information of this sort, and the arrangements for notifying people of useful news need to be prompt — a daily or weekly service rather than a monthly one, for instance.

*Selectivity* The ability of the service to supply notifications of material which matches a client's interests is important. We are talking about the ability of a CAS to *recognise* relevant, useful material. A prerequisite is detailed knowledge of the client's work and interests. Subject knowledge or experience on the part of the information worker helps recognition of potentially useful material, because the worker does not have to rely on spotting 'subjects' or keywords, and because it gives the client some confidence in his ability to help. Good selectivity is also dependent on scanners' keeping up with changes in the work of their clients.

*Content* Notifications of potentially useful material need to contain enough information about the item for a client to decide whether it is worthwhile obtaining and reading the original. A title, author's name and source reference is seldom enough.

*Ease of use* The arrangement of lists and bulletins and the reading load presented to the client by a current awareness service are crucial considerations, as is ease of access to the original material. In providing a current awareness service, we are giving the client extra work to do, and if the cost is too high, the client will make no use of it.

### Levels of service

A service which satisfies all these requirements is a rare and beautiful thing, but it is not appropriate in all cases. In fact it is possible to give CAS at several different levels of cost and effectiveness, and a level should be chosen which is appropriate to the needs of the clients and the available resources. Frequently CAS is operated at more than one level in the same information unit.

At a basic level CAS is given without the library or information department being involved in any scanning or selection of items to be notified. Examples of this approach are circulation of primary journals and other material, provision of the contents pages of current material, or provision of an alerting service produced somewhere else, and bought in. At this level the information department saves the cost of scanning and searching through the current primary literature. On the other hand, information staff have no regular contact with the current literature in the subject areas of interest to their clients, and so are not able to build up a mental picture of what is going on (which can be very useful in retrospective search and enquiry work). The client has just a part of the current literature drawn to his or her attention.

At a less basic level, library or information staff can scan current material on behalf of their clients, and send them notifications of items which seem useful for their work or interests. A list of references can be produced — called an information bulletin — or individual clients may be sent personal notifications — called selective dissemination or SDI. The cost of CAS at this level is mainly the cost of scanning current material, unless a lot is spent on printing as well. The chief benefit to the clients is that specific items known to be relevant to their work or interests are brought to their attention, saving them the time and effort of finding the relevant current literature, and going through it looking for useful items.

Some clients will use a current awareness service as a back-up to their own reading, and others will rely on it to keep in touch. There are several benefits to the information department. A regular current awareness service to clients is in fact an advertisement for the information service. Also in order to give CAS at this level the scanners will need to know what their clients are doing. This information is also useful in knowing what to collect for the library, and in the detailed planning of services. The scanning required to produce a CAS keeps the scanners in touch with what is going on in the areas of interest of their clients, and brings to their attention products, services and sources of information which are of help in connection with an enquiry service. Information staff who are obviously in touch with what is going on outside can engender much more confidence in their clients than staff who are merely seen as passing on references to them, or making outside services available, and so will be able to do more for them.

### Journal circulation

Circulation of journals and other material can be effected by the 'pass the parcel' method. A list of those who have asked to see a periodical regularly is attached to the current issue, and this is sent to the first person on the list with an injunction to pass it on when the issue has been read. An obvious problem with circulation of the library copy of a journal is that it is not available in the library. It cannot be seen by clients other than those on the list, and it is difficult to trace an issue on circulation that is needed urgently. A popular solution is to put the library copy on display for, say, a week, then circulate it. With this method, clients with a passing interest in the journal, or with a particular need to see something in just this issue, can be invited to add their names to the circulation list.

To increase the chance of being able to trace the whereabouts of a journal issue which is needed while on circulation, the 'ball game' technique can be used. Here each client returns the issue to the library after reading it. The library then sends the issue to the next client on the list.

Journal circulation involves some part of (or all of) the effort of a single member of staff, especially if one person is made responsible for checking-in new issues and tracing the whereabouts of required issues, as well as their preparation and routing. Another aspect of the cost of journal circulation is the cost of the extra copies of the more popular journals which have to be bought to guarantee that the service is reasonably timely. Six people on a circulation list is perhaps a useful maximum.

From the client's point of view this approach to CAS does not give comprehensive subject coverage, and of course it is restricted to one type of material, except where a journal carries -abstracts or reviews. On the other hand, for professional workers with a fairly narrow interest, the regular receipt of one journal may be all that is required to keep them up to date. However it is not unknown for some clients to request as many as 40 periodicals to be circulated to them. One should not be too dismayed by this. It could be that the client is on the look-out for facts or ideas to help with his or her creative work, and there is not much that a scanner could do to help. For clients to whom timeliness is important, journal circulation can be a mixed blessing. Those at the top of a circulation list can certainly be informed quickly about newly published facts and opinions.

## Contents pages

The contents pages of publications in which the clients have an interest are sent or circulated to them, and they are invited to visit the library to see any items of interest, or to ask for a copy of the item. Contents pages can be sent when the material arrives, but more often they are cumulated into a weekly or monthly bulletin.

This means that the current issues of periodicals, or other material notified in this way, can be kept in the library, where they are available to clients and information staff. However, the costs of contents page bulletins may be as high as those of journal circulation, especially if copies of articles are supplied for private study.

Clients obtain wider coverage of the current literature than is obtainable from reading a few journals. It is a more timely alerting service for most clients, and they can make their own selection, instead of relying on a scanner's selection, as with a bulletin of selected titles. On the other hand, they do have to rely on the authors' titles to guess at the subject content. Many periodicals have articles and news items which are not listed in any detail on the title page. If clients are interested in the advertisements or editorials, title pages will not be suitable either.

## Alerting services from outside

At a basic level it is possible to give a current awareness service by purchase and display or circulation of alerting publications produced by another institution. These may be commercial ventures, or they may be prepared for the clients of some other information service, but offered outside on subscription. They are designed for personal purchase and use, but many libraries and information services manage to make use of them as an intermediary. They include contents page bulletins, information bulletins from scanning primary literature, and bulletins of references from bibliographic databases.

A subscription to one of these services is a cheap way of obtaining current information. However, the effectiveness of a CAS from a single copy displayed in the library is often very low. A more effective dissemination can be obtained by sending a copy to clients known to be involved in the subject area covered, or by using the alerting publication as input to one's own current awareness service, saving on scanning the publications it covers.

*Current Contents* publications consist of the contents pages of journals in a named subject area, photocopied and reproduced as a booklet. The publications of this type from the Institute for Scientific Information in Philadelphia often arrive in one's department before the library has received the journal issues it contains. Several university departments and other specialised institutions produce current contents services, and it is worth enquiring of institutions in one's subject area. The ISI publications include the addresses of authors, so that a source of a reprint is available. Alternatively a copy of an article can be obtained from ISI's tear sheet service.

Bulletins of references to recent articles on a particular subject area are available mainly from libraries and information centres, but there are also commercial ventures of this type available, including a few on-line bulletins. In a case where the same public information is useful to the clients of information services in many similar institutions, it makes sense to buy and make available such a service from outside — for example a bulletin on higher education topics of interest to administrators in universities and polytechnics, or a bulletin on local government affairs to municipal council executives. Information bulletins bought in from outside are also used to supplement industrial information services, but here the bulletin is more likely to be produced at a research association or by an independent publisher. This is because although industry can make use of such bulletins, no one company would want to sell its bulletins to others active in the same area, revealing to them its interests of the moment.

The extent of coverage of the current literature by someone else's bulletin has to be discovered. Sometimes a list of titles scanned is published with an issue, or can be obtained. Also it has to be remembered that a bulletin from outside will seldom cover all items in any one issue of a periodical, the items notified will usually be a selection.

The producers or agents for bibliographic databases usually supply what amount to specialist topic bulletins in a variety of standard subjects. These are fundamentally different from the information bulletins referred to above, because they contain references or abstracts from the secondary literature (abstracting and indexing services) and because the items are selected by computer search with words and wordstems. The advantages and disadvantages of the secondary literature as input to current awareness service, and of computer search as compared to human search, are listed in the section on sources of items for current awareness.

These specialist topic bulletins are often obtained for a specific individual or group among one's clients, but can also be used for input to a CAS, as a back-up to scanning the primary literature.

### Information bulletins and SDI

At a different level of CAS, information workers scan the current literature, with a knowledge of the work and interests of their clients, and supply them with references to items which they feel to be potentially useful. An information bulletin is a list of such references, which is supplied as a list to a number of clients. It may contain lists of other things, like library accessions, for instance. (SDI is a more personal service — each client receives notifications of just those items which seem useful to him or her.) Thus a wider coverage of different types of literature is involved than in the techniques described above. Also the responsibility for selection of items is the information worker's, not the client's. This means that CAS at this level cannot be very successful without knowledge of the clients' work and interests.

The benefit for the clients, in addition to the value of any information or ideas they may obtain, is that they spend less time on scanning current material, if they are in the habit of doing so. If the client is not a literature-conscious person, or is never able to spare the time to go through current material, then the benefit of a current awareness service is that the client has an input to their work which would otherwise not exist.

The cost to the client is the time spent looking through a bulletin or SDI notifications, and in following up and reading items which appear to be potentially useful. This is for some quite a high cost to pay, especially if time has to be set aside 'from their work' to make use of a CAS. For this reason time and money spent in making current awareness services easy to use is well spent.

The cost to the library or information service is mainly the cost of scanning the current literature. There are benefits to the service as well, however. The information about clients' work and interests which is obtained in order to give CAS at this level is useful in collection development and in the detailed planning of services. Also current publications contain details of other potentially useful new material, and give the scanner a view of the current state of the art which is useful when enquiry work or searches have to be undertaken.

A major benefit of current awareness service at this level is one of communication. The information workers are obliged to notice the clients. The clients have a regular reminder, in the shape of the output from the service, that the library and information service is there, and may be useful.

## Sources of items for a current awareness service

Where items for a CAS are obtained by scanning the current primary literature, it is advisable not to attempt too much. The value of such scanning lies in the ability of the scanner to recognise useful material, so preferably scanning should be more detailed than running one's eye over contents pages, although this is obviously the best way to scan research journals and other types of publication with little or no editorial content. Thus the scanning needs to be concentrated on those publications likely to contain the most items on the topics of interest – the so called 'core literature' of the subject. These are the materials that a traditional library would acquire for its collection anyway. Also, a scanner should ideally not attempt to handle more than about 50 periodicals when spending about one-third of his or her time on scanning. (These figures are intended to give a rough idea of the sort of workload that has been found to result in a good-quality service with regard to timeliness and selectivity.) One has to remember that journals and trade magazines are only the backbone of the primary literature, and that other types of material will need to be collected and scanned – for example, the proceedings of meetings and conferences, reports of work elsewhere and in one's own organisation, and edited books containing state of the art reviews or a series of articles, are all very useful sources. In addition, according to the needs of one's clients, other material like patents or newspapers will need to be included in the scanning programme.

There is no rule which says that one must own material before scanning it. CAS is often given from material read in or borrowed from other libraries. Similarly items for a CAS can be read in an on-line publication. The obvious step of copying to one's own system items to be used in an in-house service is attractive if a large amount of in-house keyboarding is thereby saved. However a licence fee may be required if someone else's text is being used.

Secondary materials (printed abstracting and indexing services or their associated databases) can be used to supplement primary sources in a scanning programme, or they can be used as the main source of items. They are useful to *supplement* scanning of primary material in the following ways:

To extend coverage beyond the 'core' literature of a subject. They are especially useful when more or less complete literature coverage is required, for instance when every mention of one's company's products in the journal literature must be picked up.

To cover material in other languages in abstract form, because the original material is not bought and scanned.

To cover types of material that would be difficult or expensive to collect and scan in-house, for example, patent specifications.

Abstracting and indexing services or bibliographic databases can also be used *as the main source of items* for a CAS, to replace as much as possible in-house scanning. However, the quality of the service inevitably suffers. There are a number of reasons for this:

Where timeliness is important, it has to be remembered that bibliographic databases report a reference and usually an abstract of items from the primary literature from 12 weeks to over a year after its publication. The few exceptions relate to bibliographic databases which are able to obtain and process records of items in some primary journals in advance of these journals being published — where the producer of the database is also the publisher of the journals, for instance.

Secondary services, by their nature, do not contain references to news items and much of the editorial content of journals and trade magazines. This applies to most technical a + i services, although there are of course databases which consist mostly of references to news material, and a few of these are subject oriented, not general, in scope.

If secondary bibliographic services contained references to all items in the primary literature of their subject, they would be very much larger than at present. In fact, most contain only a selection of items, even from the primary journal literature. The better services have a selection policy which one can enquire about. This may include a guarantee of inclusion of *all* items from a list of important journals. Most secondary services can supply a list of periodicals scanned for the service. The larger services publish a list of all sources used.

A large proportion of the material discovered by searching a secondary bibliographic service is found to be unavailable in one's own library, and has either to be obtained from outside, at some cost in money and access time, or ignored. In this connection it is difficult or impossible to decide on the quality of primary publications from a title and abstract.

The relevance to a client's work and interests of an item seen in a secondary service is often impossible to judge from the title, and even abstracts can be curiously unhelpful in revealing enough about the original to enable its relevance to be guessed at. This means that one is passing on references to the clients on a subject basis, rather than because they have some perceived relevance to his or her work. Before undertaking CAS entirely from secondary services, it is as well to consider whether in the circumstances this matters.

If databases are to be used to obtain material for CAS, another set of problems arises to do with computerised search. Instead of a human eye and brain scanning text, we have a machine looking for the co-occurrence of words and wordstems listed in a 'search profile' with which it has been supplied. (There are many comparisons of searching

8

for references in secondary sources by hand and by computer. Some which are relevant to current awareness service are reported by Ashmole, Blick, Johnstone, Kiewitt, Lancaster and Miller.):

A proportion of irrelevant material is found, containing the words but not the sense of the concepts expressed in the search profile.

Material which is there in the database, and which is relevant to the clients' interest, is lost because it does not contain the words in the search profile; or because it contains them, but not in the combinations specified in the search profile.

It is difficult or impossible to draw up an effective search profile for some topics: for instance, for methods, unless they have a name. Similarly 'good' tests or investigations cannot be selected. Where a search for a group or class is needed, each individual has to be specified in addition to the group name. For instance, a search for analgesic drugs would have to specify a long list of trade names and systematic names and synonyms in the search profile. In some cases the output to a search would be heavily contaminated with false combinations of the words in the search profile. For instance, a search for items on fish effluent would find mainly items on the effect of effluent on fish.

Perhaps the most disquieting finding is that a search of the current file of a bibliographic database and a scan of the corresponding primary journals do not seem to produce much material in common!

To sum up the usefulness of secondary services, it should be said that if they are to be used *as the only source* of current awareness material, then timeliness is by no means the greatest problem if a quality service is to be maintained. They will not cover all the material relevant to clients' interests, they provide notification of material to which access is difficult or very slow, and whose relevance can usually only be discovered when it has been obtained from outside. If the references are to be obtained by machine searching of a database, some useful material will almost certainly be missed. In relying entirely on secondary sources to supply references for CAS, information workers lose the advantages of contact with the current literature. As a supplement to scanning primary material in the area of interest of one's clients, secondary services are most useful to extend coverage, and to handle types of publications that would be difficult or impossible to collect and examine on a large scale, like patents.

### Clients' interests and current awareness service

Knowledge about the work of one's organisation is crucial to the success of any sort of CAS. For a service to individuals by means of personal notifications, this must be detailed knowledge if the client is to be aided at all. The ability to recognise relevant items during scanning, and the decision about whether to notify the client depend heavily on detailed knowledge of his or her work and interests.

There is no doubt that talking with the professional workers in one's organisation is the best way to obtain enough information about their work to enable useful material to be recognised. Also a bond is formed and, if the information worker is seen to be knowledgeable and responsive, some confidence is engendered as well. Other approaches to obtaining useful information are as follows:

Reports of projects undertaken, or future plans can be read. Meetings can be attended, where the information worker can hear about what is going on in the organisation, and get some idea of the relative importance of staff in the communication/action network. In an organisation where project work is done, a meeting with the project group may lead to the possibility of a useful contribution being made.

An approach to individual clients can be made by memo, which says something about the proposed CAS, and asks them to submit a list of their interests. People tend to reply at a level of generality which is not useful, and to give an incomplete list of interests. A request for the client to write a *paragraph* on each interest can produce much more useful detail. Having the client send some articles with special relevance to his or her interests can also be helpful.

Some guidelines for interviews with prospective CAS clients may be helpful. First of all, try to find out about all the activities where current information may be useful. What research is the client doing, are there any administrative duties or committees on which he or she sits, is the client studying for a higher degree, is a series of lectures being prepared? Then obtain more detail on the client's interests. What aspects of a subject are important to the client? In his or her professional work, what materials, methods and processes are used? Obtain a description of the piece of work on which the client is currently engaged, and ask about the problems. Ask about possible threats or advantages to the work from outside.

Lastly, obtain information that could make the provision of a CAS easier. Is the client looking for technical or commercial information? Is a theoretical or practical approach to the subject needed? Are there any sources that *must* be included? Can the client supply keywords or synonyms for the more important ideas? Is timeliness important? Is more or less complete coveraged required?

Although their interests can change quite frequently, clients do not normally hasten to inform the provider of an information service when a new interest is begun. For this reason some effort has to be put into keeping in touch with clients after the initial contact. If a record of clients' interests is kept, as when a personal notification service is given, this can be sent to the client every few months or so, with a request for amendments to be made. Other channels which are useful for keeping up to date on clients' interests are meetings — either formal meetings or talking to clients over coffee, requests for literature searches, and reports of new work programmes planned. It is fatal to the success of a current awareness service just to wait until you hear from the clients. Examples of techniques for maintaining interest profiles can be found in the report of Whitehall's (1979) survey.

### Current awareness notifications

A notification of an item selected as of potential interest to a client needs to do more than tell the client that this item exists. It should also contain enough information for the client to decide whether or not to read the original. This may seem an obvious comment to make, but the fact is that it is a common experience among users of a CAS that references to items in the primary literature, or copied from secondary bibliographic sources are found not to be helpful in this way. Clients' reactions to such items in bulletins are either to ignore them, to wonder why the item was included, or in some cases to send for a copy or visit the library to find out. Unfortunately not all clients feel that they have the time to check on the relevance of items.

A notification which is a reference should at least contain a title, author's name, date and details of the source. If this is a periodical, inclusive pagination should be given, so that the client knows the length of the original. Some indication of where the material is available is helpful. If the title of the item is general or uninformative, a few words of explanation should be added, to indicate what aspects of the topic are covered. For an in-house service, based on a detailed knowledge of the clients or client groups, the annotation can be written in quite a pointed way, to show just what it is in the item that is considered potentially useful. Where current awareness service is given at a distance, to people the information worker sees seldom or never, it is better to write or pass on abstracts which indicate all the main ideas covered in the item. Collison's book contains very helpful advice on writing abstracts.

A type of notification which avoids to a great extent the problem of leaving the client to guess at relevance, and which does not involve the information worker in writing annotations, is to pass on the first page of the selected item.

If the item is short, or if it is a news item, the first page of it may be the whole. If not, the client can obtain the rest of the item if it seems relevant. Page copies are commonly used for personal notification services.

Where items selected for a current awareness service are presented as a bulletin, one or two features connected with ease of use and relevance are worth considering.

Printed bulletins should be slim and attractive. Ideally they should not be so large that they represent a separate reading task to the recipient, or they may be laid aside until he or she has time to deal with them. For a busy person, this may be never. An attractive bulletin has the advantage that it does not disappear on the recipient's desk by merging with the other papers there. It stands out because of its cover or first page or coloured mast-head.

Bulletins should have an easy-to-read arrangement. Short bulletins of one or two pages tend to be read from start to finish, so that the order of items is not critical. However, a longer bulletin could usefully offer the client an option for selective reading. Sectionalisation by subject is a common feature of larger bulletins — but it cannot be stated too strongly that the subject indication scheme should be simple, and the clients should be aware of the indication policy, and agree with it. An extension of this approach is to have a separate bulletin for each 'subject', and to invite clients to choose their own mix of these SDI bulletins. Sectionalisation by journal title is an alternative method of presentation, which reflects the normal approach of professional people to the literature. It is also possible to combine these methods by printing a bulletin containing items in journal order, with subject codes added in the margin against each item. An on-line bulletin, which the clients reads at a terminal, can be even more flexible in that it can offer a choice of end-to-end scanning, scanning by named subject sections, or search by combination of words in titles or other text. (Rogers discusses examples of on-line bulletins in her chapter in Chapter 6.)

Another feature associated with ease of use of a CAS is the procedure for requesting a copy of an item for private study. This can be made easier by allowing the client to indicate an item on a numbered list rather than requiring him or her to write out full bibliographic details for each and every item.

### Production of current awareness services and a database

It may be felt necessary to build up a database for retrospective search purposes containing items put into a bulletin or SDI service. This might be done for material such as internal reports, which will not appear in commercial databases, and so cannot be searched for there, or for material which, although it is publicly available, needs to be indexed in a way not possible through the use of on-line secondary services. In the interests of cost-efficiency, the activities involved in current awareness notification and database production should be integrated as far as possible.

Such databases are often indexed by addition of words from a thesaurus to the record of each item, to give easy access by the concepts of special interest to the users of the database. Another well-tried technique is to produce and maintain a rotated title index of items. In this case words in the title are marked as keywords, and words and phrases are added to the title when it does not indicate concepts which need to be retrievable. The point is that as far as possible indexing decisions should be made at the time of scanning, and the keyboarding of the items for current awareness notification should include any codes or additions which are necessary in the production of the database.

Selection of a method for combining current awareness notification and database production has to be done with care, to ensure that requirements for both outputs are met. Whitehall (1979) discusses integration of the activities, and supplys a non-computerised method for producing a bulletin and a rotated title index (1972). Green and Whiting have used SUPERFILE and WORDSTAR for production of bulletin and index on a microcomputer. Golland's chapter in this book describes the use of ADLIB for this purpose. Other relevant software is listed by Rowley. There is a great deal of this sort of activity going on in libraries and information departments, and the best advice is to find someone who has a system running and go and see it before spending money on machines and software.

### References

Ashmole et al., 'Cost-effectiveness of current awareness sources in the pharmaceutical industry' *J. American Society for Information Science*, January–February, 1973, 29-39.

Blick, A. R. et al., 'A comparison of on-line databases with a large in-house information bulletin in the provision of current awareness, *Journal of Information Science*, 1982, vol. 4 no. 2/3, 79-86.

Collison, R. L., *Abstracts and abstracting services*, ABC-CLIO Press, Santa Barbara, Calif., 1971, 3-17 and 26-7.

Green, K.E. and Whiting, J., 'Combined production of a current awareness bulletin and a database on a microcomputer', *Program*, October 1984, 298-307.

Johnstone, S. M., 'Choosing between manual and on-line searching – practical experience in the Ministry of Agriculture', *Aslib Proceedings*, October–November 1978, 383-93.

Kiewitt, E. L., *Evaluation of information retrieval systems*, Greenwood Press, 1979.

Lancaster, F. W., 'A study of current awareness publications in the neurosciences', *J. Documentation*, September 1974, 255-72.

Miller, J. K., 'Two methods of providing selective dissemination of information to medical scientists (manual SDI versus ASCA profiles)', *Bulletin of the Medical Library Association*, July 1970, 378-97.

Rowley, J. E., 'Bibliographic current awareness service – a review', *Aslib Proceedings*, September 1985, 347.

Whitehall, T., 'An integrated non-mechanised system for information bulletins and a keyword index', *Unesco Bulletin for Libraries*, July–August 1972, 193-213.

Whitehall, T., 'Personal current awareness service: a handbook of techniques for manual SDI', British Library R & D Report 5502, September 1979.

# 2

# The choice is yours!
# Choosing the best method
# for current awareness provision

*Alan Blick*

The provision of current awareness to a community of customers by an in-house information service or special library is generally accepted as highly desirable. It has long been one of the main roles of industrial information services and special libraries. The value or popularity of current awareness provision has been demonstrated[1,2] and it is difficult to envisage how, for example, a research department in a high-technology area could function without a good awareness of the relevant current literature.[7]

However, although the desirability of current awareness notification is well accepted, there is virtually no consensus on what is the best method of providing such current awareness notification. The literature contains many reports of evaluations of current awareness services and even some comparisons of alternative approaches[3,4], but the literature does not, and cannot, provide a definitive answer on the best method to choose. The reason for this is the variety of methods available and the variety of environments in which current awareness is to be provided. It is obvious that the method most suited for providing an individual with current awareness on a narrow well-defined subject with no need for good timeliness would not be the most suitable method for providing a large community of research scientists working in a wide, diffuse subject area with a premium on timeliness. The method of current awareness must suit the environment in which it is to be provided and must relate to the information resources (staff, equipment, material and financial) available.

## Alternative methods for current awareness

A selection of alternative methods of providing current awareness is given below. It is by no means an exhaustive list.

1.  Journal display
Current journals received in a library can be displayed as a routine in a library. Customers can browse amongst the display to maintain a current awareness.

2.  Journal circulation

Current journals circulated amongst customers provide the source material for current awareness.

3.  Contents page circulation

The distribution of photocopies of contents pages of journals on display in the library adds a notification feature to alternative 1.

4.  Bought-in SDI

Several commercial organisations offer the service of providing notification, usually as computer output, of new items of literature on a specific topic.

5.  In-house SDI

SDI services equivalent to those provided by commercial organisations can be provided in-house by the information department. They can be provided manually or by mechanised methods (e.g. on-line profiles).

6.  In-house bulletins

Information bulletins can be produced by the Information Department, either manually or using mechanised techniques.

7.  *Current Contents*

The ISI publications containing contents pages of current issues of journals are well established as a current awareness notification method.

8.  Bought-in macroprofiles

Similar to bought-in SDI but much broader in subject area covered, macroprofiles are produced by the Royal Society of Chemistry, by Derwent Publications Limited and other commercial organisations.

9.  Do-it-yourself reading groups

Users can participate in current awareness provision by identifying for their colleagues items of relevance in the journal literature as they read it. The identified items can be culled and produced as a bulletin, or other methods can be used to bring the items to the attention of their colleagues.

**Criteria for assessment of alternatives**

Below is listed a range of criteria by which the alternative methods can be compared. Again, it is not an exhaustive list. Any information manager or special librarian can add other methods of current awareness provision or assessment criteria which may be relevant to their environment. What most cannot do, however, is find the time to make a detailed comparison of all the alternative methods before deciding on which to choose. The luxury of having the time to spend on such comparisons is rarely found outside the information science research profession. Information science researchers can make objective comparisons of the methods and provide techniques for such comparisons[5], but they cannot take into account during their researches the environmental factors pertaining in an individual information department which affect the decision on what method to choose. The information manager must therefore be cognizant of the investigations and their findings and must then overlay the environmental factors.

Criteria for assessment of alternative methods of current awareness provision

1.  Timeliness
In some organisations there is a need for immediate notification of relevant items in the literature; in other organisations timeliness is not so important. Different methods of current awareness have marked differences in timeliness.

2.  Source coverage
It is generally desirable to be as comprehensive as possible in coverage of the literature for current awareness item selection.

3.  Selectivity
In some situations it may be desirable for the current awareness service to select only substantial items and to ignore minor or trivial items.

4.  Relevance
In any set of current awareness notifications, a high degree of relevance is desirable. However, total relevance suggests less than total recall and a compromise must be reached between relevance and recall.

5.  Abstracts available
The presence of abstracts in a current awareness service can be of considerable value and convenience to the user.

6.  Full paper available
The provision of the full paper as the current awareness notification provides the user with the maximum information on that paper.

7.  Readability
Some computer output is unsympathetically arranged for readers, some is excellent. Different approaches to current awareness notification produce different qualities of print and ease of reading.

8.  Cost
The cost of the provision of the current awareness service should include labour, material, equipment, computing and subscription costs, plus any ancillary costs.

9.  Special equipment or resources
If the information unit or special library has to buy or lease

equipment such as a word processor or microcomputer in order to provide the service, then this is an important consideration.

10.   Staff time

Staff time affects cost. However, it is also important that the amount of staff time absorbed by the current awareness service should be appropriate to that available in the unit.

11.   Customer interaction or feedback

In some types of current awareness provision, it is possible to design user feedback into the service.

12.   Suitability for large groups of customers

In organisations with many potential users of the current awareness service, it is important that the method of current awareness provision chosen should be suitable for a large number of readers.

## Choosing the best method

A simple method which can be used to help choose the most suitable method of current awareness is to score the degree of success of each alternative in meeting each of the specific criteria. A total score for each alternative against all the criteria can be obtained, and the alternative with the highest score should be the most appropriate method for current awareness. An early description of the methodology is reported in[6], but the method is illustrated in Table 1.

On the left-hand side of the grid the table lists alternative methods for current awareness as described. Across the top of the grid are the criteria for assessing alternative methods. One horizontal column has been completed to illustrate the technique. The scores are given out of ten. As an exercise the reader may like to complete the remainder of the grid for his or her local environment.

It is not suggested that the completion of a comparison grid such as shown in Table 1 will provide the perfect answer. What completing the grid does is enforce a discipline into a method of comparison which is appropriate for the manager of an information unit or special library. The scores entered can be deduced from product literature, from commercial current awareness providers and from the manager's own knowledge. The methodology recognises that a lengthy detailed investigation of all the alternative methods is impractical. It exploits knowledge acquired from general information work and does not require extensive investigation or research.

### Completing the grid

The example chosen as the method of providing current awareness in completing the grid is *Current Contents*. This is a well-known journal contents page publication, produced by the Institute for Scientific Information (ISI), which is widely used for current

## Table 1
## Alternative forms of current awareness and criteria for their evaluation

| Score 1 to 10 The higher the score, the nearer the method meets that criterion. | Timeliness | Source coverage | Selectivity | Relevance | Abstract available | Full paper available | Readability | Cost | Special equipment/ resources | Staff time | Customer interaction or feedback | Suitable for large group of customers | Total score (120 possible) |
|---|---|---|---|---|---|---|---|---|---|---|---|---|---|
| 1. Journal display | | | | | | | | | | | | | |
| 2. Journal circulation | | | | | | | | | | | | | |
| 3. Contents page (copy) circulation | | | | | | | | | | | | | |
| 4. Bought-in SDI | | | | | | | | | | | | | |
| 5. *In-house SDI* (A) Manual | | | | | | | | | | | | | |
| (B) Mechanised | | | | | | | | | | | | | |
| 6. *In-house bulletin* (A) Manual | | | | | | | | | | | | | |
| (B) Mechanised | | | | | | | | | | | | | |
| 7. Current contents | 9 | 8 | 2 | 4 | 0 | 0 | 3 | 9 | 10 | 9 | 1 | 5 | 60 |
| 8. Bought-in macroprofiles | | | | | | | | | | | | | |
| 9. DIY reading groups | | | | | | | | | | | | | |

19

awareness. It has substantial strengths and weaknesses as a current awareness method. Some of these are discussed below for each criterion in the grid. The reader may well think of other factors relating to each criterion. The points discussed are meant to be illustrative rather than exhaustive.

*Timeliness*: One of the strengths of *Current Contents* is that it is generally very timely. Its production process is simple and fast. It is produced almost embarrassingly quickly, as frequently items appear in *Current Contents* before the journal containing the item has been received by a lending library such as the British Lending Library. The user therefore can know of the item before his library can obtain it (unless the library uses the rather expensive OATS services associated with *Current Contents*). *Current Contents* therefore scores very high on timeliness. A score of 9 out of a possible 10 is allocated in the grid against this criterion.

*Source coverage*: *Current Contents* contains the contents pages of over 1,100 journals. The number of journals covered by *Current Contents* is several times greater than the number of journals taken by the average industrial library. Consequently the score for coverage is high. It is not the maximum because other publications and/or databases (for example *Chemical Abstracts*) have even greater coverage in specific areas. Score 8.

*Selectivity*: The score for selectivity is low. There is no selection in *Current Contents* based on the merit or substance of an item. All items in the contents page of a journal are reported in *Current Contents*, regardless of merit. There *is* an inherent selectivity in that usually only journals of substance are covered by *Current Contents* and therefore trivial items in trivial journals are not included. This moves the score away from zero. Score 2.

*Relevance*: A variety of *Current Contents* are produced by ISI, referring to the journals in specific subject areas such as behavioural sciences, clinical practice, physical, chemical and life sciences. This selective coverage of journals means that for the user there is a relevance factor in these *Current Contents* publications. However, it is a relatively small relevance factor when compared with the high degree of relevance which can be achieved by an information specialist selecting items whilst journal scanning or by a computer profile. Score 4 for relevance.

*Abstract available*: There is no abstract of any kind available with *Current Contents* and so the score is zero.

*Full paper available*: The full paper is not available to the reader in the document he receives as current awareness and so the score again is zero.

*Readability*: Regular users of *Current Contents* will be surprised to see a score as high as 3 out of 10 for readability. *Current Contents* is not easy to read although it has improved appreciably over the years. It is not as bad as some computer-printed current awareness outputs, however, and deserves a score above zero for its improvements. It is in a very portable form, suitable for reading on trains or in planes, which also scores to its advantage.

*Cost*:   *Current Contents, Life Sciences* has a subscription cost equivalent to around £5 a week. This is a remarkably low cost for current awareness provision from such a large journal list. Many of the alternative forms of current awareness provision such as bulletins or computer profiles would cost much more than this. £5 is probably less than the cost of producing one abstract for an abstract-based bulletin. It is accordingly given a high score of 9 against the cost parameter.

*Special equipment/resources*:   No special facilities such as on-line computer terminals, or even a typewriter, are required to use *Current Contents*. (It is probable that after using it for some time reading glasses will be required, but it would not be fair to score this against it.) Therefore as no equipment of any kind is involved in the use of *Current Contents* as a current awareness facility it scores a maximum of 10.

*Staff time*:   No more time is involved in obtaining *Current Contents* than is required for the average journal on subscription. If multiple copies are obtained they must be despatched to the individuals requiring them, but the total effort involved is very small in comparison with alternative current awareness methods. Score 9.

*Customer reaction or feedback*:   It can be very useful to be able to build some form of customer feedback into the current awareness service. Such feedback can give evidence of features such as degree of relevance. It is not easy to build user feedback into *Current Contents* as it is produced in a ready-to-issue form. An in-house bulletin, for example, could be purpose-designed to embrace this feature. Therefore *Current Contents* scores low on this parameter. Score 1.

*Suitability for a large group of customers*:   A single copy of *Current Contents* is most unsuitable for a large group of customers. It takes an appreciable amount of time to scan and it would take a long time to circulate around a large number of readers. It would also lose its merit of timeliness in the process. However, it is understood that multiple copies of *Current Contents* can be obtained from ISI at discount rates. This goes some way to making it more suitable, as the purchase of multiple copies would overcome the circulation problem. A score of 5 is given against this parameter because *Current Contents* can be made more suitable for multiple users, but at the cost of multiple subscriptions.

*Total score*:   *Current Contents* achieves a score of 60 out of a possible 120 on the basis of the arguments used above. Other current awareness alternatives could score quite differently. The alternative with the highest total score when the grid has been fully completed would be the option to choose.

The above method of scoring assumes that each parameter has the same importance in the decision-making process. This may or may not be the case. Two parameters which may have much greater importance than the others in a small library or information unit are 'cost' and 'staff time'. If the financial resources of a small unit are very limited, then the money spent on current awareness provision could have a substantial impact on expenditure or on other aspects of the service.

It is up to the manager of the unit to decide where his priorities lie and he may decide to spend a large proportion of his budget on current awareness. However, in such a unit, choosing a low cost method of current awareness provision would be sensible, as it would not swallow up a large proportion of the budget. The parameter of cost should therefore be given a greater importance than other parameters. The same reasoning can be used for staff time. In a small unit, staff time is usually at a premium and it is unlikely that a small unit would commit substantial staff resources to producing a current awareness bulletin if an alternative existed which required very little staff effort (for example, *Current Contents*). Therefore the parameter of staff time should be given extra importance in comparison with other parameters. This can be achieved by weighting the parameters. That is, at the time the grid is drawn up the parameters of paramount importance are allocated an importance of, say, 1.5 x or 2 x the importance of the other parameters. The dimension of importance can be determined only by the person making the decision. Thus, in a small unit, if the score of 5 is given to a method of current awareness against cost, this score is increased to 5 x 1.5 or 5 x 2, depending upon the importance allocated to cost. In the example of the grid previously used the decision that 'cost' and 'staff time' are twice as important as the other parameters would change those particular scores for *Current Contents* to 9 x 2 = 18 and 9 x 2 = 18. The total score for *Current Contents* would then be increased from 60 to 78.

Consideration of the individual parameters will reveal that different environments could lead to different parameters being of especial importance and appropriate weighting would have to be applied accordingly.


## Conclusion

A wide range of alternative methods of providing current awareness exists. The average librarian or information practitioner does not have the time or resources to perform detailed comparisons of these alternatives, but must make a decision on which one to use. A crude, simplistic approach to making the choice is by the method described.

If necessary, weightings can be applied to take account of especially important parameters.

The method is far from ideal. Its value lies in formalising the decision-making process and avoiding the need to make a decision based on intuition or personal bias.

## Notes

1.  Warden, C. W., 'An industrial current awareness service. A user evaluation study', *Special Libraries* 1978 vol. 69, no. 12, 459–67.
2.  Blick, A. R., et al. 'The value of a weekly in-house current awareness bulletin serving pharmaceutical research scientists', *Information Scientist* 1975, vol. 9, no. 1, 19–28.
3.  Blick, A. R., Gaworska, S. J., Magrill, D. S., 'A comparison of on-line databases with a large in-house information bulletin in the provision of current awareness', *Journal of Information Science*, 1982, vol. 4, nos. 2/3, 79–86.
4.  Chaloner K. et al. 'A comparison of two current awareness methods', Proceedings, 43rd ASIS Annual Meeting, *Communicating Information* 1980, vol. 17, 90–3.
5.  Francis, G. M., et al., 'A manual for the evaluation of current awareness bulletins', *BLRD Report* 5584 1981.
6.  Blick, A. R., 'Evaluating an in-house or bought-in service', *Aslib Proceedings*, 1977, vol. 29, no. 9, 310–19.
7.  *Current awareness: principles and practice*, AIOPI Occasional Series, 3, July 1985.

# 3 Information bulletins produced on a co-operative basis

*Alan Blick*

The majority of current awareness bulletins are produced by a single library or information service based in a single location. Some organisations, however, are spread across multiple locations and the question arises whether or not the current awareness bulletin should be produced (a) centrally by one site, (b) individually at each site, (c) co-operatively across all sites. This chapter will discuss option (c): a current awareness bulletin serving several sites or locations and produced by those sites in co-operation.

The literature provides very little in the way of accounts of bulletins produced co-operatively from several sites. Two relatively recent accounts[1],[2] discuss bulletins produced co-operatively in two very different environments. The first services local government in Yorkshire and district and is based on public libraries. The second serves research scientists and is based on a multi-site research division of a pharmaceutical company

## Choice of option

The decision on whether to service a multi-site organisation with a current awareness bulletin produced (a) centrally by one site, (b) individually at each site or (c) co-operatively across all sites is influenced by a variety of factors. The factors include whether or not each site has its own library/information service.

If only the central site has a library/information service and the other sites do not have library/information services, then it is impractical to produce a bulletin by option (b) or option (c) as these sites would either not have their own bulletin or would not be able to contribute to a co-operatively-produced bulletin. If the subject interest of each of the sites is unique unto itself and there is no overlap of interest across the sites then option (b) would appear to be the one choose. More usually, the situation lies between these two extremes. That is, in a multi-site situation it is common for several of the sites to have library/information services, if only of a satellite nature, and it is almost inevitable that work done at one site is of interest to one or more of the other sites. In this situation all three options for the production of a current awareness bulletin are possibilities.

In the following discussion four basic assumptions are made. The first is that it is highly desirable that the person selecting items for an information bulletin should have a sound, up to date knowledge of the interests of the readers of the bulletin. This knowledge is necessary regardless of whether the bulletin is produced by selection of items from literature scanned in-house or by the use of profiles to select from computer-based sources. Without such knowledge the selection of items is likely to be inaccurate, incomplete and inadequate. The second assumption is that it is highly desirable for the information specialist to be motivated to perform the act of item selection. A badly motivated person will not be conscientious in the selection of items and is unlikely to be active in keeping aware of the changes of interest of customers.

The third assumption is that the production process of the current awareness bulletin, including all the activities involved, should be as cost-effective as possible. The fourth assumption, and perhaps the most important of all, is that the customers should want to receive the bulletin and should feel it is relevant to their interests.

### Option (a) A bulletin produced centrally by one site

*Advantages* There is something essentially tidy and appealing about a central site, probably with a substantial information resource, producing a current awareness bulletin serving all other sites within an organisation. The concentration of the activity in one place can mean staff can be committed full time to this specific activity, the production process is controlled within one unit and so is easy to run, and overall the management requirement of the bulletin is modest and clearly defined.

A bulletin produced from a central site is the sole responsibility of the library/information service on the site. Decisions regarding changes to the bulletin design, content and frequency can be made without the need to consider other library/information services within the organisation. Communications from users regarding the bulletins can be directed to the one central service.

*Disadvantages* The main, overwhelming disadvantage of a bulletin produced from a central site lies in the remoteness of the source of the bulletin from its users at other sites. This remoteness from the users makes it extremely difficult for the information specialists compiling the bulletin to be accurate and comprehensive in their selection of items for inclusion. The remoteness from the user makes communication of changes of interest and research topics slow and difficult. Users can be invited to notify the central site immediately when their interests change but in practice this is unlikely to happen. More probably, the distant user will become dissatisfied with the lack of relevance of the bulletin to him personally and will develop a jaundiced view of it.

Publications received at remote sites which have been issued by a central site have a resentment barrier to cross which does not exist for locally-produced publications. This resentment lies largely in such centrally-produced publications in reality constituting a one-way communication process. Even though the opportunity may exist for return communication, actually stimulating and obtaining feedback is very difficult. This lack of feedback can be dangerous as it can lead the central site information specialists into believing that, owing to lack of comment, the bulletin is well received, when in fact the reverse may be the case.

The motivation of the information specialist will be only modest. They will be producing a bulletin for sites they may never visit and for readers they may never see. Changes in topics for selection, when they are notified, will not be achieved by a chat with a customer face to face, but remotely, by telephone or letter.

### Option (b)   A bulletin produced at each individual site within the organisation

*Advantages* The main advantage of current awareness bulletins produced individually at each site reflects the main disadvantage of option (a). That is, a locally produced bulletin for a specific site can react quickly to changes of interest among its customers. Communications between users and information specialists, as they are on the same site, can be, and should be good. Accuracy of selection of items for the bulletin should be good and the user should feel that the bulletin has him in mind.

The fact that the bulletin is produced locally rather than remotely appeals to its recipients who feel they can influence it directly and immediately.

The information specialists producing the bulletin have the gratification of knowing that their work is being directed to their local users. Their motivation to produce a good bulletin should be high, leading to better job satisfaction than in option (a). The production process will be completely under their control.

*Disadvantages* There is much in favour of bulletins produced individually at each site of an organisation and the disadvantages are not as substantial as for option (a). The main disadvantage of option (b) is duplication of effort. There is little doubt that the production of a bulletin at each of several sites duplicates the production process several times. In addition, if there is overlap of interest across the sites there is either duplication of content in the bulletins to cater for this overlap, or the bulletin from one site will be sent to other sites to provide current awareness in the overlap area.

The duplication of content in the various bulletins is wasteful of time, effort and materials. However, attempts to overcome it by sending the bulletins produced by individual sites to other sites raises other problems. These problems include inflicting more than one bulletin on the user, the circulation of several different bulletins of different design and format, the inconvenience to the users and the site libraries of bulletins of varying timeliness, and an overall loss of sense of image for the corporate information service.

### Option (c)    A bulletin produced co-operatively by several sites

*Advantages* Although not necessarily the main objective of a current awareness bulletin produced co-operatively by information specialists working at different sites, one of the main advantages is the unifying effect it has on the corporate information service. The production of a bulletin in this manner involves frequent communication amongst the information specialists across the sites. Ideas originating at individual sites can be used for the common good. At the same time the information specialists retain their commitment to the local site customers and serve as their contact point. A co-operative bulletin produced correctly should overcome any problem of duplication of content. At the same time the relevance of the appropriate part of the bulletin to any one user should be as good as in a bulletin compiled locally. Overlap of interest across the sites will be catered for because users will have access to all parts of the bulletin in which they have an interest.

The production process will be a single procedure with no duplication of effort in customer liaison, scanning or bulletin duplication.

*Disadvantages* A co-operatively-produced bulletin with input originating at different sites which must be brought together for a certain deadline can, initially, be a little complicated to control. Changes to the bulletin format, production schedule, coverage and so on must be agreed across all the sites which contribute to it. In practice, a competent secretary or clerical assistant can manage the routines of the production of a co-operatively produced bulletin with little difficulty.

### A procedure for a co-operatively produced bulletin

The procedure described below relates to option (c): an information bulletin which is produced from input from information services staff across several sites. The bulletin is envisaged to be a large, multi-section bulletin containing items of relevance to research workers at the various sites. The items in the bulletin consist of title, author and journal source. (No abstracts are given with the items but this is not a feature which must be excluded from a co-operatively-produced bulletin. Abstracts can be incorporated with no real impact on the overall production system other than a deterioration in timeliness.) A similar approach can be adopted for other types of bulletin, such as a

Future Events Bulletin containing notification of conferences, meetings, seminars etc.[3] The production process of a co-operatively produced bulletin can be described in terms of the main features listed below. Other features figure in the process, but these are the features which, if managed correctly, should ensure the successful production of the bulletin: appearance, user subject interest, bulletin item selection, typing or keyboarding, user section requirements, printing, and distribution.

### Appearance

One of the main advantages of a co-operatively-produced bulletin is to give the staff of the information units across the sites a feeling of belonging to a unified corporate information service. In addition, a well designed information bulletin can engender a good corporate image for the information services across all the sites. It makes the users aware that the whole service is bigger than the part of the service on their site with which they interface, and that the information resources are much larger than just those operated on that site. Consequently the appearance of the bulletin should be good. It should indicate that it is produced by the information service but it should not refer to any particular site. A brief text on the front cover should explain that it is produced for all sites from input from all the individual sites.

### User subject interest

In order to produce a relevant bulletin it is necessary for the people selecting items for it to have a sound, up to date knowledge of the users' needs and interests. At each site the information specialists are responsible for obtaining this information from their users. The information is usefully compiled into subject profiles so that other information specialists on that site, or newly recruited ones, can use the profiles as guides. The information specialists at different sites must communicate to each other changes in the interests on that site.

When the bulletin is first designed, and at periodic intervals afterwards, information specialists from different sites must come together to discuss how the bulletin is to be formatted and who is to supply the items for the different sections of the bulletin. Some sections of the bulletin will be highly specific in subject content and will relate predominantly to the users at one site only. Other sections of the bulletin will be more general and will relate to two or more sites. The selection of items, (by manual or computer-based techniques), on topics specific to a site will be made by the information specialists at that site. The selection for the more general topics will be made from all sites. The responsibility for the selection of input to the bulletin could end up as shown below:

28

| Subject area | Selecting site |
|---|---|
| Section A (specific topic) | Site 1 |
| Section B (specific topic) | Site 3 |
| Section C (specific topic) | Site 4 |
| Section D (general topic) | Sites 1, 3 and 4 |
| Section E (specific topic) | Site 2 |
| Section F (specific topic) | Site 1 |
| Section G (specific topic) | Site 4 |
| Section H (general topic) | Sites 2, 3 and 4 |

When the bulletin is first introduced, and whenever changes are subsequently made to it, all recipients of the bulletin should be sent a brief definition of the subject coverage of each section of the bulletin. This enables them to recognise which sections will be relevant to them, which will be of interest, and which it would be a waste of time for them to receive. They then select the sections they wish to receive. For example, a user on Site 4 may choose to receive sections C, F and D. Section C would be highly relevant to him whereas the F and D sections probably would be of general interest. The user would almost certainly *not* wish to receive all the sections in the bulletin.

The flexibility of approach which allows the users at all sites to choose whichever sections are of interest to them, no matter which site has input the items, is one of the main advantages of a co-operatively-produced bulletin.

### Bulletin item selection

The methods used for the selection of relevant items from the literature for use in an information bulletin are varied and can range from manual scanning of new issues of journals to the downloading of relevant items from on-line databases and subsequent computer-generation of a bulletin. The best method depends upon staff resources, user needs, subject area and other factors (see Chapter 2). The method chosen for this example of a co-operatively produced information bulletin is manual scanning. That is, items are selected by the information specialists by scanning new journals, *Current Contents* and other material collected by the library.

On each site, each information specialist is aware of the subject interests on that site. A selection of the incoming journals and *Current Contents* are scanned immediately on receipt by any one information specialist and all journals are scanned by someone. As the bulletin exemplified does not contain abstracts, the marking of relevant items can be extremely simple. If an item in a journal should be selected for Section A, then 'A' is marked on the contents page. If an item should be input to Section D, then all that is necessary is to mark 'D' against that item on the contents page. If an item is of relevance to Section A and Section D then 'A' and 'D' can be marked on the contents page against the item. All items marked 'A' are then typed in Section A, all marked 'B' in Section B and so on. When an information specialist finds an item which is for a bulletin section covered by all sites then the contents page is marked accordingly and a copy of this contents page is sent to the site which finally collates the bulletin. At this site the marked contents pages which bear duplicate items are removed before a bulletin section is typed. Such duplication occurs only when the same journal is scanned at more than one site, and so is relatively easy to control.

This method of marking items for a bulletin makes minimal clerical demands on the information specialist and makes the scanning procedure relatively quick.

### Typing or keyboarding

In order to produce the bulletin a 'master' must be produced for subsequent reproduction. This can be achieved either by direct typing on to a sheet suitable as a master or by keying the items into a computer for subsequent regeneration in bulletin master form.

If no suitable computer facility is available the bulletin master for each section is produced by typing all the items marked 'A' on the Section A sheet, then typing all the items marked 'B' on to the Section B sheets and so on. This is a rather inconvenient procedure for the bulletin typist, although very straightforward. A better procedure is for the typist to be able to type all items as she receives them into a computer system, regardless of which section they are for. The item is flagged with the bulletin section code on input, and the computer later regenerates all the 'A' items together on one sheet, all the 'B' items on another sheet and repeats this for all the sections. An added attraction of computerised compilation is that the items can be used to build an in-house database of bulletin entries for subsequent retrospective searching.

The bulletin 'master' sheets are produced by the typist weekly, or to any other predetermined frequency. A cut-off date is agreed for the production of the bulletin issues, and all items received from the information specialists prior to that date are produced on the masters.

### User section requirements

As explained in the previous section, users can request any combination of the bulletin sections. In one such bulletin[2] there are over 25 sections. This makes the permutation of possible combinations of sections enormous. (This situation exists regardless of whether or not the bulletin is co-operatively-produced.) It causes problems in the collation of the bulletin and generally means it must be assembled by hand.

One quite simple procedure can help in bulletin collection. Pre-printed self-adhesive labels can be produced which are address labels for a user but also carry his section details (see below). An address label is stuck on a bulletin front cover, which is then used to identify which sections to attach for that user.

| | |
|---|---|
| DR. J. SMITH | |
| B23 | Sections A, B, F, H |
| Site 3 | |

The selection of sections by a user will reflect the work the user is engaged in on a particular site. However, almost certainly the user will wish to see some bulletin sections which relate to the work done at other sites, either because that work is related to his own work or because he wishes to maintain an interest in that area. In addition, if any sections are produced which are of general interest in content, then such sections will be requested also. The end result should be that the specific interests of any individual user on any site are met and the associated and general interests are provided for also.

*Printing*

The printing of a co-operatively-produced bulletin is a simple matter and does not differ from any other sectionalised bulletin. A record must be kept for each section of how many copies are required. (Different sections will be required in different numbers dependent upon the users' requests.) This is a simple record-keeping procedure but should be performed at the site responsible for collating the sections of the bulletin.

*Distribution*

The distribution of the bulletin obviously depends upon the facilities within the organisation. An effort should be made to ensure that users at all sites receive the bulletin on the same day to avoid any site feeling the poor relation. Use of the pre-printed address labels previously mentioned can obviate the need for addressing envelopes. It is the responsibility of each site to ensure that their users receive the bulletin and to initiate new orders and cancel bulletins no longer required.

31

The production process for any information bulletin needs alert supervision. Bulletins despatched to users who have left the company or who no longer wish to receive the bulletin, or bulletins sent to users containing sections they do not want, creates an unfavourable image for the Information Service. If the unwanted or inappropriate bulletin is delivered week after week, then week after week the image of the information service is damaged. It is important therefore to have good administrative control of a bulletin production process.

This is more important, and a little harder to achieve, when the bulletin is produced on a co-operative basis. In addition to ensuring appropriate bulletins are sent to the right people, there is a need to maintain the bulletin schedules. That is, all the input from the different sites must be received by the administrator of the system on the same day. This input must be collated, and duplicate items in sections containing input from more than one site must be deleted before the whole is assembled for despatch for printing. This collation may simply be a matter of bringing together the different typed sheets for the different sections. Alternatively it may require bulletin input in a computer format, for instance floppy discs, to be obtained from all the sites, read and sorted on the computer, and output in sectionalised bulletin form.

Controlling a bulletin of this nature means time must be spent on the collection and collation process, records must be kept of the addresses of users and their section requirements, address labels carrying these section requirements may have to be produced, and an overall awareness of how the system is operating must be retained. This overall control can be achieved by a suitable secretary or clerical assistant but the need for effective management of the bulletin system should not be underestimated.

### Comment

The reasons for and against producing a bulletin on a co-operative basis as opposed to producing it centrally, or individually at each site have been discussed. There is no doubt that the production of a co-operative bulletin is a practical proposition. Whether or not it is the best way to meet the current awareness needs of a multi-site organisation depends on various factors. The main objective of any information bulletin is to provide notification to users of new relevant literature, and a bulletin produced on a co-operative basis can undoubtedly achieve that. What such a bulletin can also achieve, if operated properly, is an appreciable contribution to the unification of information units physically separated at different sites and even, to some extent, a unification of the user community across the sites. This could be a significant contribution achieved by the production of a bulletin on a co-operative basis.

## References

1.  Duckett, R. J., 'YADLOGIS: A Success Story in Co-operation', *Aslib Proceedings*, 1977, vol. 29, no..1, 158–67.
2.  Blick, A. R. and Magrill, D. S., 'The Value of A Weekly In-house, Current Awareness Bulletin Serving Pharmaceutical Research Scientists', *The Information Scientist*, March 1975 vol. 9, no. 1, 19–28.
3.  Forward, M. E. and Selby, M. A., 'Forthcoming Events Bulletin', *Aslib Proceedings*, August 1978, vol. 30, no. 8, 298–301.

# 4 Use of an external computer database in the production of a current awareness bulletin *

*C. J. Want*

## Introduction

STC Technology Ltd (STL) is the principal research centre of STC plc. Prior to 1982 STC was a fully owned subsidiary of the American based multi-national ITT Corporation (formerly the International Telephone and Telegraph Corporation). Since October 1982 ITT has retained only a minority shareholding in STC. STL carries out research and development in software, electronics, telecommunications and related materials. In addition to other STC management companies, its customers include, for example, ITT, British Telecom, UK Ministry of Defence and the EEC. The company employs approximately 1,000 staff at its site in Harlow, Essex, over half of whom are graduate enginners or scientists.

The Central Library and Information Service at STL forms part of the Information Resources Department, which, in addition, contains an editorial and technical word processing section. Although resourced to serve the needs of STL, the service has for some years also had the responsibility of acting as a central facility for the rest of STC and associated companies, acting on a strict cost recovery basis. The stock of the library includes 12,000 books, 10,000 reports and 13,000 slides, and the library subscribes to 500 journal titles. Normal current awareness services of a special library are provided, covering the report, journal and book literature, including: the display of current issues of journals, accessions lists, current awareness bulletins, distribution of contents pages of journals and selective dissemination of information. Patents current awareness is the responsibility of the STC Patent Department. The library and information service has a staff of 9, four of whom are professionally qualified librarians or information scientists.

**History of STL current awareness services prior to use of an external database**

From 1960 the STL information service provided a current awareness service of the journal literature through the publication of a central current awareness bulletin for STC entitled *Library Circular*, which was an annotated titles bulletin arranged by subject headings, published weekly by scanning the 300 journal titles then received by the library. With the relentless growth of the literature this outgrew the manual means of production being employed. The situation was temporarily contained by employing a much stricter selection procedure and to reflect this greater selectivity the *Library Circular* was superseded by *Selected Current Titles*.

In 1968 an ITT-Europe (ITTE) Information Network was set up to co-ordinate information activities in ITT companies in Europe. A new titles-only current awareness bulletin named *Documentation* was launched in 1969, published by STL, with the intention of replacing the six separate bulletins then being published by different ITTE companies, and to provide a service for the first time to those companies which had no current awareness service. From the outset this was conceived as a computerised bulletin and a suite of programs was specified and written in-house to run the bulletin on the in-house mainframe. Input for the bulletin was obtained by scanning journals at STL, and to a lesser extent at the associated French and German companies of ITTE. Input to the mainframe was by paper tape prepared on paper tape typewriters. Originally this data preparation was carried out in the STL typing pool but was subsequently moved in-department. The references were sorted by the computer and appeared under one, two or three of approximately 100 subject headings. Authority lists of subject headings and journal abbreviations were held on the system. Output was initially via paper tape to a paper tape typewriter and later via magnetic tape and magnetic cassette to a composer using proportionally spaced fonts. By 1976 the number of journals being scanned at STL was 600, and there was an average of 275 references per issue of *Documentation*, with a world-wide distribution of 1,500 copies.

From 1975 a second specialised bulletin was published, on the subject of printed circuits using the same computerised process. Input for this bulletin was obtained by scanning primary and secondary sources. The bulletin was distributed to a separate circulation of 700 specialists.

**The need for change**

Two forces necessitated a change in the means of providing a current awareness service. There was the increasing growth in the literature which was relevant to ITT and there were problems with the in-house production of the bulletin.

Within the service, it became increasingly difficult to assign the information staff time necessary for scanning the journals; proof-reading; progressing the computer runs; progressing the preparation of the camera-ready copy; progressing the printing of the bulletin and performing its distribution.

In addition, outside the service, there were problems in obtaining rapid progressing through the computer department. The use of lower case printing on the line printer was at that time a non-standard application requiring special processing, and the use of paper tape input and output became increasingly non-standard. As a result the computer runs were assigned a low priority. Similarly, program changes required as a result of operating system and other changes received the low priority typically given to in-house customers. The typesetting was carried out by a separate department off the main site and this inevitably provided further opportunities for delays in the production cycle.

The length of the production cycle adversely affected the timeliness of the bulletin. The delays in the production cycle affected the regularity of publication.

However, it was considered, particularly in view of the size of the distribution, that some form of bulletin remained the most appropriate form of current awareness. From 1972 the possibilities of producing the bulletin by means other than manual scanning had been investigated with the intention of achieving as many as possible of the following objectives:

(a)  to provide a service more efficiently in terms of time and cost with the emphasis on saving staff time;
(b)  to provide broader and deeper subject coverage;
(c)  to provide more regular publication;
(d)  to provide a more current service.

The possibility of using commercial databases as an alternative to in-house scanning was investigated. *Documentation* had traditionally concentrated on the electrical and electronic interests of ITTE, and INSPEC was therefore considered to be the database most likely to be able to replace manual scanning. An investigation of six months' data showed that INSPEC covered 66 per cent of the journals scanned by STL and included 50 per cent of the references selected for *Documentation*. The three main possibilities investigated were:

(1)  the distribution of reprints or photocopies of sections of *Science Abstracts*;
(2)  running INSPEC tapes in-house;
(3)  production by INSPEC of a bulletin from the INSPEC and ISMEC databases.

Following an initial costing exercise in co-operation with INSPEC, it was decided to proceed with the third of these, together with the publication of a supplement to cover the references not being included in the INSPEC database.

As the manual bulletin was judged to be largely successful it was the intention that the INSPEC produced bulletin should be broadly equivalent to it in terms of layout and subject arrangement, although any incidental improvements would be welcome. Targets of an overall relevance of the bulletin of 60 per cent and a recall of 75 per cent of the relevant references in the INSPEC database were set.

## Methodology of bulletin production from a commercial database

### Survey of other services' solutions

A survey of the current use of external databases for the production of current awareness services revealed a range of methods of application. Some current awareness bulletins have been produced by the database producers themselves. INSPEC, at that time, were producing *Current Papers*, a titles-only version of *Science Abstracts*. (The range of services from INSPEC has subsequently been increased so that as well as selective dissemination of information (SDI) services they now also produce *Key Abstracts* and a standard profile SDI service *Topics*.) Similarly NASA were producing bulletins in fairly narrow subject categories using standard SDI profiles.[2,12,14]

In his 1972 survey, Whitehall[15] found that 44 per cent of his sample of information services were using external services for current awareness, 18 per cent of the total using printed publications. Although some information services were able completely to replace an internal bulletin by published services[8] a number of services were producing supplementary bulletins to cover specific interests not included in the published service.

As an alternative to using complete published abstracts journals the distribution of *Chemical Abstracts* subject groupings has been found to be a feasible solution.[10]

Another method was the production of bulletins from abstracts supplied by an external service. Over 12 per cent of Whitehall's sample who were providing a current awareness service were using this method. A further step in the same direction was the central production of bulletins by, for example, research associations. In 1969 RAPRA were producing 12 such bulletins on behalf of their members, selecting references either using a subject profile or on the basis of journal titles.[6] However, by 1976 only one of these was extant.

Yet another method was the production of bulletins based on the results of regular online searching of computer databases. An example of such a bulletin was *Atlas Biomedical Condensates*, a twice-monthly bulletin produced by scanning copies of original articles, the references to which had been retrieved on-line.[11]

On the basis that it should be cheaper to produce bulletins from databases than to produce SDI services from them, the Experimental Information Unit at Oxford experimented in 1971 with the production of two such bulletins, *Gas Kinetics* and *Electrolytic Solution Bulletin*.[4] *Gas Kinetics* was produced from *Chemical Titles* using an author, journal and keyword search and from Automatic Subject Citation Alert (ASCA) using authors only. The bulletin did not outlive the experiment. The *Electrolytic Solution Bulletin* was produced using a keyword and citation search on ASCA. This bulletin was still being produced in 1976 but 30 core journals were then being scanned manually, supplemented by predominantly citation searches on ASCA.

A similar philosophy was used at the Biomedical Documentation Center, Karolinska Institute, to produce *Pollution Lookout*, using searches in *Biological Abstracts, Bioresearch Index, Chemical Abstracts* and *Medlars*. This ceased publication in 1976 and was replaced by *Teratology Lookout* published by editing the output of on-line searches on *Chemical Abstracts Condensates, Biosis Previews* and *Medlars*.

Overall the production of bulletins from computer databases by performing SDI-type searches did not appear to have produced bulletins of very great longevity. Moreover, manual editing of the computer search output was usually found to be necessary.

*Means of selection of items from the database*

For the STL current awareness bulletin a total of nine different methods of selection were considered and investigated. The abstracts journal *Science Abstracts*, the printed output from the INSPEC database, was used in the investigations. A detailed account of the investigation has been published elsewhere.[13].

Initially the possibility of carrying out an SDI search to select references for each of the 100 bulletin headings was considered. However, this was rejected on the basis of cost and the staff time necessary to maintain the profiles. A less selective means was then considered, that of using complete *Science Abstracts* subject sections. This was rejected on the grounds that the subject sections gave too low a precision for the needs of the bulletin because the INSPEC subject sections were, in general, much broader than ITTE interests.

In order to achieve a higher selectivity, some means of selecting references from within the subject sections was sought. By marking up references which were judged to be relevant by the information staff within a subset of the subject sections of *Science Abstracts*, and analysing the number of relevant and irrelevant references from each journal title appearing in those sections, it was possible to rank the journals in terms of their 'precision' (the proprotion of articles they supplied of interest to ITTE). An improved precision for the bulletin as a whole could then be obtained by using a broad selection of subject sections and 'high precision' journals, that is, selecting only from journals with a 'precision' above some given value. The resulting bulletin precision and recall, however, proved unacceptably low (precision of 69 per cent at a recall of 49 per cent and 55 per cent at a recall of 75 per cent).

The effect of selecting references in the selected subject sections only from those journals already subscribed to by the STL library was then investigated. However the maximum recall possible was only 66 per cent, at a bulletin precision of 30 per cent. In order to improve the recall, a number of the highest ranking journals from the list of precision-ranked journals were added to the selected journals, sufficient to give a recall of 75 per cent. This gave a precision of only 41 per cent at a recall of 75 per cent, compared with the precision of 55 per cent at 75 per cent obtained using the complete precision ranked list of journals.

Instead of selecting journals from a precision ranked list, the possibility of using a recall ranked list was then investigated. Using the broad selection of subject sections and high recall journals the bulletin precision was found to be almost independent of recall, with a precision of less than 50 per cent corresponding to a 75 per cent recall. This level of bulletin precision was judged to be unsatisfactory.

The possibility of moving the higher selectivity from the journals to the subject sections themselves was investigated. By reducing the number of subject sections to a third of the previous number and placing no restrictions on the journals or other forms of literature from which the references were selected, a total recall of 79 per cent was obtained, but at a precision of only 37 per cent. A further refinement of the selection of subject sections was introduced in an attempt to improve the bulletin precision. The sections were ranked by precision, in the same way in which the journals had previously been ranked, and only the highest ranking sections used. Using these high precision subject sections and all forms of literature gave the highest precision to date for all values of recall, with a precision of 56 per cent at a recall of 75 per cent.

A final refinement was the use of a precision ranked list of *Science Abstracts* subject headings and a precision ranked list of journals. By using this combination of precision ranked lists and appropriate cut-offs on the two lists it was possible in the pilot study to obtain a bulletin precision of 62 per cent at a recall of 75 per cent.

*Production of selection list from the whole database*

Having arrived at a *modus operandi* in the pilot study, the method was applied to some months' data over a wide range of subject sections believed likely to contain relevant references, in order to obtain lists of sections and journals to be used in the bulletin. The analysis was carried out first on the subject sections. Relevant references were found in 404 of the 531 sections studied and the highest ranking 283 of these sections were chosen, the lowest having a section precision of 28 per cent — corresponding to a recall of 87 per cent.

Using the selected list of subject sections, three months of abstracts journals were studied to obtain a precision ranked list of journals. Of the 2,400 journals covered by INSPEC in 1976, relevant references were found from 565, and 459 were above the initial cut-off. The list was refined using additional data to resolve the position of those journals accepted in the initial list on the basis of 'insufficient data to be significant'. By showing that additional data would reduce their precision, 33 journals could be removed from the list, and by showing that additional data would add further relevant references, 57 journals had their inclusion in the selected list confirmed.

The selected list of journals differed significantly from the list scanned for the manual bulletin. For example, foreign language journals made up 24 per cent of the journals on the selected list compared with 6 per cent foreign language journals scanned for the manual bulletin.

Of the 700 journals scanned for the manual bulletin 310 were not included in the selected list. Of these only 133 were scanned by INSPEC for the database. Requests for original papers from the journals represented 26 per cent of the requests received by the STL library for photocopies in a six month test period. A small number of journals contributed a relatively large number of these references, and INSPEC agreed to consider including these journals in their coverage.


*Test of the selection method*

As a test of the selection method, the relevant references in an independent month's secondary journals were marked up, the whole of the secondary journals being scanned and not just selected sections. Determinations could then be made of the recall and precision obtained using the select list of subject sections and journals. The figures obtained were a recall of 52 per cent, and a precision of 41 per cent. The recall and precision failures were investigated separately.

Recall failures could arise in unselected sections or in unselected journals within selected sections. Three-quarters of the relevant references which were not recalled were in unselected sections. A considerable proportion of these came from selections which had not been scanned in the preliminary analysis. As a result a net total of 33 sections were subsequently added to the list of selected sections. A third of the recall failures were caused by the journal selection. Seventeen per cent of the total recall failures were from journals which had not been considered in the analysis, either because those journals had not appeared in the database in the analysis period or they were new journal titles or changes of title.

Taking into account the recall failures which were from unconsidered sections or journals, the effective recall from the considered sections and journals was 75.2 per cent, which met the target of 75 per cent. It is obvious that in the determination of subject sections the net must be thrown more widely than had been the case in the original analysis, and that the journal list would need to be updated frequently to account for changes in the journals included in the database. INSPEC subsequently agreed to include automatically all straight-forward changes of title from titles included in the original list.

The determination of recall and relevance is obviously dependent on the determination of relevance of the references. In the original analysis of the database the overall relevance of the considered sections was determined to be 11 per cent, while in the test period the overall precision of the same sections was 6 per cent. It is to be expected that this difference, whether genuine or caused by different criteria of relevance, will result in a reduced precision of a bulletin produced by selections from those sections. If this change in precision is uniform across the sections it would be sufficient in itself to account for the difference in the achieved and target precisions.

However, in order to improve the bulletin precision it was decided to introduce a manual editing stage in the production cycle to delete irrelevant references. This was found to require two man-hours a week. With subsequent tuning of the selected lists of sections and journals, and with experience of the wide range of requests for original articles being received by the library, it was subsequently found possible to dispense with this editing step.

### Subject concordance for the new bulletin

The intention was that the INSPEC produced bulletin should, as far as possible, use the same subject headings as had been used in the bulletin from manual scanning. It was therefore necessary to construct a cross-reference list from the selected sections to the bulletin subject headings, and this proved possible with only minor changes to the existing bulletin subject headings.

In the INSPEC database, references may be assigned more than one classification code (corresponding to subject sections in *Science Abstracts*). Since in general more than one classification code may be mapped to a bulletin subject heading, it would be possible for references to be duplicated under a given heading. INSPEC built in a procedure to prevent this. The same reference might still appear under more than one bulletin heading by mapping from different classification codes but this was consistent with the practice in the manual bulletin.

Twenty-four of the existing subject headings in the manual bulletin had no classification codes mapped to them. Some of these headings were too specific for there to be a corresponding classification in INSPEC and some were outside the range of INSPEC's subject coverage.

### Implementation of the new bulletin

References were extracted from the database by using the SDI procedures. The selected list of journal titles and *Science Abstracts* subject sections was used as a profile to run against the weekly SDI tapes, thus giving the optimum timeliness. An output tape was produced of the hits, which was subsequently used to produce the print masters for the bulletin. The production cycle therefore followed the stages: selection from the SDI tapes, production of a line-printer proof run for manual editing; external film production as print masters; checking and correction; external printing; transport of printed sheets to STL for making up and distribution. Contents pages were made up manually. In the initial issues the average number of references per issue was 434, an increase of 35 per cent over the number in the manual bulletin.

The production of six-monthly cumulations of the bulletins was abandoned with the transfer from a manual to the INSPEC-produced bulletin. These cumulations had been used for information retrieval within the department, but since all the references in the INSPEC bulletin were available on the INSPEC database on the commercial on-line systems, it was decided to rely on these for information retrieval in the future.

### Documentation *supplement*

The selected list of journals for the INSPEC bulletin did not include 310 journals which had been scanned for the manual bulletin, and in a test six-month period 26 per cent of requests for copies of papers had been from these journals. A small number of journals which had contributed a relatively large number of references to the manual bulletin were within the subject areas covered by INSPEC and they agreed to consider their inclusion. However, in addition, some ephemeral papers which would have been chosen from the selected journals were not included in the INSPEC database. In order to notify users of papers not included by INSPEC it was necessary to publish a supplement. Originally this was produced on the in-house mainframe using the same procedures used for the complete manual bulletin. Production was subsequently transferred to a computer bureau to remove the delays inherent in being an internal customer to the in-house computer. Subsequently a Wang word processor was installed in the department for performing the cataloguing function and for main-taining a mailing database and the supplement production was transferred to the word processor to bring all the cost in-house and further reduce the time delays.

In the final Wang word processor production method the weekly data for the supplement was input to a List Processing file, using codes for journal titles and the subject headings under which the reference was to appear. The abbreviated journal titles and the full subject headings were held as separate indexed List Processing files. BASIC programs were written to expand and sort the input data under up to three subject headings and, via word processing, to produce camera-ready masters.

The camera-ready masters from the word processor were used to print the supplement in-house and were then collated with the main bulletin pages from INSPEC.

There were an average of 176 references per issue in the supplement, and with the final in-department system a timeliness of 22 days from receipt of the journal to publication of the bulletin was achieved.

### Experience of using an external database

*Changes in the bulletin*

In changing from an in-house bulletin to one produced from a commercial database, a number of relatively minor changes to the bulletin were necessary. These included a small reduction in the number of subject headings in the main bulletin corresponding to headings which had no corresponding subject sections in the database, and an initial increase in the proportion of non-English language journals.

The format of the bulletin was similar to that of the INSPEC current awareness bulletin *Current Papers*. As a result, authors' affiliations were included with the bibliographic details for the first time. It had not been considered cost-effective to do this with the manually scanned bulletin but here was a bonus received from using the database, and it was appreciated by a number of users. There were also incidental typographical improvements in the bibliographical details corresponding with the usage in the INSPEC publications. Different forms of journal abbreviations were used in the INSPEC database from those used internally at STL. It had been felt that this might cause some difficulties for library staff, but in fact there were no significant problems.

References also appeared in a different order in the INSPEC produced bulletin from the order which had been used in the manual bulletin: within each section they were in approximate alphabetical order of journal title rather than in author order.

The overriding advantage achieved with the INSPEC-produced bulletin was regular publication. There were however disadvantages in terms of timeliness and precision. The timeliness achieved with the

INSPEC bulletin from receipt of the same issues of the journals at STL was an average of 82 days compared with the 42-day target for the manual bulletin; the supplement was finally published in less than 21 days. The average precision of the first issues was 47 per cent compared with the 100 per cent precision (measured by the same criteria) of the manual bulletin.

The precision of the bulletin was also monitored in terms of the requests received at the STL library for copies of original papers. This is not exhaustive since some users would use local company libraries to obtain papers or would read the papers within the STL library without generating a recordable request. It was noted that there were a significant number of requests for papers which would not have been included in the manual bulletin, as interest in the particular topic was unknown to the information staff. This demonstrates the advantage in terms of recall of the wider net thrown by the INSPEC bulletin. In terms of precision, however, it was consistently found that the manually scanned supplement scored higher than the main INSPEC bulletin.

### Effects on the information service of an externally-compiled bulletin

There were a number of effects on the information service. The objective of freeing staff time was achieved but was not quantified because of simultaneous changes in practices within the department such as the introduction of on-line searching for information retrieval.

The problem of lack of current awareness among the information staff was anticipated by arranging that all journals were still passed to information staff, suitably marked for cursory or complete scanning. This obviously reduced the staff time savings achieved but was felt to be justified.

As experienced elsewhere when external databases were introduced[3,5,7,10] there was a considerable effect on the demand for outside loans. There was initially a marked increase but the level of demand subsequently returned to former levels by tuning the selected list of journals and the library's holdings to bring them into line.

#### Monitoring and modifying the system

As the bulletin passed into production it was necessary to establish a policy of monitoring and modifying the lists of selected sections and journals. There were three souces of changes which had to be catered for: changes in the database classification scheme; changes in journals covered by INSPEC and changes in company interests. Computer programs were written to run on the department Wang word processor to carry out the analyses necessary to maintain the lists of selected subject sections and journals in the light of these changes. As a result it was possible in these monitoring exercises to include a very much larger proportion of the subject sections in the analysis than had been used in the manual pilot study.

### Return to a manually-produced bulletin

Following the divestiture of a number of companies in Europe by ITT in the early 1980s there was a considerable fall in the circulation of *Documentation*. This became even more marked with the relinquishing of a majority interest in STC by ITT and a consequent scaling-down of the ITTE Information Network activities. At the same time there had been a steady increase in the use of SDI services as an alternative to the use of the bulletin by the library users. As a result the circulation of *Documentation* had fallen from 1,500 in 1976 to 350 by the beginning of 1984. Because most of the costs were independent of the number of copies issued this resulted in a commensurate increase in the annual subscriptions charged for the bulletin and at this level it was no longer economic to maintain the production of the bulletin based on the external database. The decision was, therefore, made to return to a bulletin produced by manually scanning the journals received at STL. At the same time the specialist bulletin on printed circuit boards was combined with *Documentation*. The combined bulletin was now produced on the department system developed for the *Documentation* supplement, so that scanning, keyboarding, computer processing and the production of camera-ready copy (using proportional spaced fonts and double column printing) were all carried out within the department. This avoided almost all the delays and problems associated with the production of the original manually scanned bulletin. It did place a considerable additional burden on the information and library staff but the staff costs involved were still advantageous compared with the use of an external database at this lower level of circulation. It was expected that the same advantages of timeliness and relevance over the use of external services would be experienced as were still being experienced elsewhere.[1,9] Although the timeliness has improved compared with the external bulletin, consistently maintaining the theoretically achievable timeliness has proved to be the most difficult objective. An on-line package has subsequently also been developed so that the data accumulated for the bulletin can also be used for in-house information retrieval.

### Summary

It proved possible to publish a co-operative current awareness bulletin with a large internal circulation from an external computer database. As a result three local bulletins ceased publication and one other continued in a modified form, scanning only journals which were not included in the co-operative bulletin.

Fortunately, there existed an external database which had a significant overlap of coverage with the interests of the company. It was also significant that the database producer was enthusiastic in pursuing the possibilities of using the external database. However, to cover topics and types of literature not included in the database, it was necessary to publish a supplement to the bulletin by manual scanning of the primary journals. This limited manual scanning was also important to maintain the current awareness of the information staff themselves.

The bulletin achieved the aims of regular publication and savings of information staff time devoted to scanning primary journals. Some staff time was necessary to review the select lists periodically, and to assist in this computer programs were developed to rank the classification codes and journals, based on the selection of relevant references from the printed version of the database. There was a reduction in timeliness of about six weeks in going from the manual bulletin to the INSPEC bulletin.

Acceptable results were obtained by using precision ranked lists of classification codes and journals to search for references within the database. The use of a select list of journals had the advantage of limiting the number of external inter-library loans necessary to meet requests once the local library subscribed to the majority of journals included in the selected list.

With a fall in the circulation of the bulletin, partly as a result of competition from SDI services, and partly as a result of a reduction of the number of co-operating companies, there was a return to a bulletin produced by manual scanning. This was possible because the information service now had a word processor and expertise in programming so that the whole publication cycle, apart from printing, could be run and maintained within the department. The production delays associated with the original bulletin produced by manual scanning were therefore avoided. In addition, the data accumulated in machine-readable form for the bulletin could be used for on-line information retrieval.

## Notes

1.    Blick, A. R., Gaworska, S. J. and Magrill, D. S., 'A comparison of on-line databases with a large in-house information bulletin in the provision of current awareness', *Journal of Information Science*, May 1982, vol. 4, nos. 2/3, 79—86.

2. Bloomfield, M., 'Current awareness publications: an evaluation', *Special Libraries*, October 1969, vol. 60, no. 8, 514—20.

3. Corbett, L., 'Problems in using external information services: attitudes of the special library and its users', *Aslib Proceedings*, February 1972, vol. 24, no. 2, 96—110.

4. Corfield, M. G., 'Experimental bulletin services', September 1971, OSTI Report no. 5113.

5. Dammers, H. F., 'S.D.I.: some economic and organizational aspects', *Aslib Proceedings*, October 1971, vol. 23, no. 10, 517—22.

6. Dawson, D. R. and Elliott, R. G. J., 'Co-operation in abstracting: part 2: from co-operation to contracts', *Aslib Proceedings*, December 1969, vol. 21, no. 12, 501—4.

7. Friend, P. D., 'The use of external data bases to extend current awareness based on internal resources at AWRE Aldermaston', *Aslib Proceedings*, December 1972, vol. 24, no. 12, 678—85.

8. Helliwell, B. F. M., 'Experiences of BP's Patents Information Branch in using commercial patent documentation services', *Aslib Proceedings*, January 1973, vol. 25, no. 1, 18—21.

9. McVicker, J. M., 'A comparison of on-line SDI with an in-house current awareness bulletin', M.Sc. thesis, City University, London, 1979.

10. Peterson, J. S., 'Replacement of an in-house current awareness bulletin by "Chemical Abstracts" section groupings', *Journal of Chemical Information and Computer Sciences*, August 1975, vol. 15, no. 3, 169—72.

11. Tillmans, E. J. H., Boylen, J. B. and Kendis, M. S., 'Atlas Bio-medical Literature System: a computerized current awareness and information storage and retrieval system', *Journal of Chemical Documentation*, November 1971, vol. 11, no. 4, 242—8.

12. Vickery, B. C., 'External sources of information: the kinds of services and facilities offered and criteria for evaluation', *Aslib Proceedings*, December 1972, vol. 24, no. 12, 664—71.

13. Want, C. J., 'Replacement of an in-house current awareness bulletin produced by scanning primary journals by an equivalent bulletin [produced] by selection of references from the INSPEC and ISMEC data bases', M.Sc. thesis, City University, London, 1976.

14. Wente, V. A. and Young, G. A., 'Selective announcement systems for a large community of users', *Journal of Chemical Documentation*, August 1967, vol. 7, no. 3, 142—7.

15. Whitehall, T., 'A future for the bulletin? The results of an enquiry into how bulletins are used in today's special library', *Aslib Proceedings*, February 1973, vol. 25, no. 2, 34—45.

Computerised current awareness
          and information retrieval:
          *Daily Intelligence Bulletin*

*Richard Golland*
*Philip Hathaway*

Since 1970 the Greater London Council Research Library has issued
a *Daily Intelligence Bulletin* (DIB) for use by councillors and local
government officers at the GLC itself and in the London boroughs.
(For a general description of Research Library services to London local
government see Golland.[1]) It is written and circulated each weekday
and consists of a single A4 sheet, printed on both sides, with about
30 summaries of news reports on topics of interest to local government.
During 1982 the Research Library began to introduce the Adlib
computerised library housekeeping package, which is created by
Lipman Management Resources Ltd of Maidenhead, UK. (A description
of the Research Library's adoption of the Adlib package has been
published.[2]) The package is mounted on the GLC's Prime 750 minicomputer, and uses specially adapted Cifer 2634 visual display
terminals. Until November 1982 DIB was produced by largely manual
methods. Since then we have used a computerised system written by
staff of the GLC Methodology Group* and the Research Library, and
which exploits part of the Adlib package. In this chapter, we describe
DIB, compare old and new procedures for producing it and comment
upon some advantages and disadvantages of the new system.

**Current awareness, information storage and information retrieval**

The elements of the DIB service are the current awareness
bulletin, the cuttings files and the indexes.
  (1) *Current awareness bulletin* (Figure 1): The main sources for
DIB are the national 'quality' daily newspapers (*Daily Telegraph,
Financial Times, Guardian* and *Times*); the 'quality' Sunday newspapers
(*Observer, Sunday Telegraph* and *Sunday Times*); and the (London)
*Standard*. When space permits, some news items from weeklies and

The Methodology Group and the Research Library are sections of the
Intelligence Unit set up by the GLC to provide information services
to London's local government. With the abolition of the GLC in April
1986 the Intelligence Unit was transferred to the London Residuary
Body and DIB production has continued.

monthlies may be included. Press notices from the GLC and from other central and local government sources are also cited frequently. About 6,000 DIB items (each of which can refer to several cuttings from different sources) are generated each year. The 'summaries' consist of selections of those points from the cuttings deemed of greatest relevance to our users. They are not exhaustive abstracts. After the summary appears a statement − in date, then journal title, order − of the sources being cited. In the left-hand column beside each summary, are (a) a unique item number, which identifies the library location of the cuttings themselves, and (b) a subject heading. The subject headings, which may be single words or phrases, are drawn from a standard list and, since summaries are printed in alphabetical subject heading order, users can scan for their own topics each day very rapidly. Subject headings are sometimes followed by subheadings, which usually indicate a geographical location. About 1,100 copies of the bulletin are distributed each day, but, since many London borough recipients then duplicate their copies for further distribution round their own town halls, we do not know exactly how many copies are finally produced.

(2) *Cuttings files*: Since 1972, all the cuttings cited have been filed in the Research Library in item number order. They can be used for reference, or individual photocopies can be made for private study. (A sample survey conducted in summer 1984 suggests that about 30,000 photocopies per year are being made by or for GLC users. Numbers of photocopies supplied by London borough libraries and information services are unknown.) There is now a collection of roughly 80,000 items reflecting the development of urban local government-related issues over the past 12 years.

(3) *Indexes*: The form these take will be described below.

DIB, then, is not just a current awareness bulletin. The bulletin is the most visible part of a substantial cuttings library system − and retrieval problems were an important element in the decision to computerise.

### Producing DIB before computerisation

What was the DIB production process like just before computerisation? Let us go back to 1982 (Figure 2). A team of five or six Information Officers (professional librarians or information scientists) is responsible for compiling DIB. Since it is extremely important to try to circulate the bulletin as soon as possible, Information Officers each buy a newspaper on the way into work − or on the way home if they are responsible for the *Standard*. This enables them to scan and select relevant reports before they reach the Library. This is not always possible, of course. Strap-hanging in a crammed bus or Underground train is not conducive to efficient scanning! On arrival

GREATER LONDON COUNCIL

Prepared in the Research Library. Edited by: Tim Owen      Wednesday November 28, 1984

Further information on any of these items is available from the Research Library. Photocopies of items listed are only provided for GLC officers outside the County Hall complex via ext 6068: for all others a self-service system operates in Room 513. London Borough officers should contact their local library service.

| 84 07633 Charities | The Home Office is to reconsider the Metropolitan Police Commissioner's authority to grant or refuse applications for street collections of money in the light of James Wood's successful challenge at Clerkenwell Court. (Police Rev 16/11 p2285) |
|---|---|
| 84 07642 Civil Liberties | In his Granada Guildhall lecture on 'The Right to Know', Lord Scarman has called for the complete repeal of the Official Secrets Act and for a new Freedom of Information Act. (G 28/11 p1) |
| 84 07640 Construction | BIA figures show that house rebuilding costs have risen by an average of 5.1% in the year to September. (BIA PN 44/84 21/11: FT 28/11 p8) |
| 84 07649 Ecology | Labour Opposition Environment Spokesman John Cunningham MP has said in the Commons that the Wildlife and Countryside Act was a failure, and called for Government grants to farmers for carrying out conservation work. (FT 28/11 p10: G p27) |
| 84 07617 Education | A BIM report 'Action on Education', has criticised the DES for under funding and failing to give a lead in forging links between industry and education. (Tel 28/11 p10) |
| 84 07622 Education | Nearly 100 Conservative backbenchers supported a Commons motion last night condemning the plan to increase parental contributions to student grants; students plan to hold a rally on the South Bank today against the DES proposals. (FT 28/11 p1,4: T p28) |
| 84 07636 Elderly | Government Statistical Service forecasts, calculated for use in long term estimates of pension costs, show that the number of pensioners in England and Wales will increase by 2.5m over the next 40 years. (G 28/11 p6) |
| 84 07644 Elections Enfield | Further report on the Enfield Southgate by-election following the launch of the campaigns of candidates Timothy Slack (Liberal) and Peter Hamid (Labour). (Tel 28/11 p10) |
| 84 07637 Environment Westminster | Westminster Council is to take on extra staff to deal with the nuisance caused by builders' badly placed hoardings and rubbish skips. (S (City P) 27/11 p15) |
| 84 07629 GLC Members | The DPP has informed GLC Director General Maurice Stonefrost that he can find no justification for asking for police inquiries to be made into the failure of GLC Member Neil Davies to declare an interest in a South Bank craft centre. (S (Clos P) 27/11 p15) |
| 84 07634 GLC staff | The GLC has admitted that Council staff seconded to the Democracy for London campaign had canvassed in council time in by-elections fought by Labour candidates in September. (T 28/11 p2) |
| 84 07646 Heliports London | The British Helicopter Advisory Board has proposed five possible Thames sites for heliports, off Whitehall, and at the Temple, Billingsgate, Butlers Wharf and Hermitage Wharf near Tower Bridge. (T 28/11 p1) |
| 84 07638 House purchase | The Building Societies Members Association (BSMA) response to the Government Green Paper 'Building Societies: a New Framework' includes a call for an ombudsman to protect members' rights. (FT 28/11 p9) |

**Figure 1.** *Daily Intelligence Bulletin*

| | |
|---|---|
| 84 07620<br>Industry<br>Wandsworth | Michael Ward, GLC Industry and Employment Committee Chair, will open the GLEB funded London Production Centre today, a production facility for London's electronics industry, to provide up to 500 jobs. (GLEB PN 79 28/11) |
| 84 07626<br>Local government<br>expenditure | Westminster City Council yesterday claimed in the High Court that ILEA's plan to spend £750,000 on an advertising campaign against rate capping was unlawful. (G 28/11 p5: Tel p10) |
| 84 07647<br>LRT | Hofmeister Lager are to provide free travel on all London bus and Underground services after 11pm on New Year's Eve until 4am on New Year's Day. Also, the Phoenix Brewery in Sussex has launched a Christmas "Get You Home" taxi service for motorists at 500 of its pubs. (S (Clos P) 27/11 p10: T 28/11 p1: Tel p8) |
| 84 07635<br>Mortgages | 'Lending in the Major Conurbations' published yesterday by Nationwide Building Society, shows that the average mortgage for house and flat buyers in London and its commuter belt this year is nearly £27,000 compared with just under £22,000 for the United Kingdom. (T 28/11 p3) |
| 84 07618<br>Parking<br>London | The LBA is to ask the Government to give London Borough councils the power to tow away illegally parked cars. (S (City P) 27/11 p13) |
| 84 07628<br>Parliament | The Lords agreed in a debate last night to a 6 month experiment in televising their House's proceedings, starting in January. (FT 28/11 p10: G p2,27: T p4,28: Tel p13) |
| 84 07621<br>Police | A GLC Police Committee report claims that Special Branch officers are monitoring and interfering in legitimate political and trade union activities; the Council plans to call for the Branch's disbandment in its evidence to the Commons committee investigating its operations. (S (City P) 27/11 p15) |
| 84 07639<br>Privatisation<br>Cambridge | A Cambridge Health Authority team investigating the dispute between cleaners at Addenbrooke's Hospital and the contractors OCS has upheld union complaints about poor training, supervision, standards and quality control. (G 28/11 p3; T p5) |
| 84 07645<br>Prostitution | The Government is backing a Private Member's Bill, to be introduced this session by Conservative MP Janet Fookes, aimed at tackling the nuisance of kerb crawling. (T 28/11 p3: Tel p19) |
| 84 07625<br>Railways | British Rail has released details of new Southern and Eastern Region timetables, to be introduced next May, for commuter services into London. (S (City P) 27/11 p10: Tel 28/11 p8) |
| 84 07630<br>Railways<br>London | The London Regional Passengers Committee (LRPC) has asked the Government to stop British Rail from closing Broad Street Station unless it puts adequate alternative tracks into Liverpool Street Station. (Tel 28/11 p13) |
| 84 07623<br>Science parks<br>Hillingdon | Planning permission for Stockley Park, a 340 acre business technology park near Heathrow, was announced yesterday by Hillingdon Council. (S (Clos P) 27/11 p5: FT 28/11 p7: G p24: T p15) |
| 84 07627<br>Sport<br>London | Dennis Howell MP, Labour Opposition Sport and Recreation Spokesman, will join Peter Pitt, GLC Arts and Recreation Committee Chair, tomorrow in a considered response to the future of sport as outlined in the Local Government Bill on abolition. (GLC PN 827 26/11) |
| 84 07631<br>Transport | Dave Wetzel, GLC Transport Committee Chair, sent a message of support to the organisers of the National Public Transport Week of Action which started on Saturday. (GLC PN 825 24/11) |

**Fig. 1 cont.**

| Time | Editor | Information officers | Typists | Clerical assistant* |
|---|---|---|---|---|
| 8.45 | Sifting selected cuttings, choosing those to be included in DIB | Scanning newspapers and selecting cuttings | | |
| 9.15 | | Writing summaries (including subject headings and source citations) | | |
| 9.30 | Checking and amending summaries, then sorting summaries of cuttings into subject heading order | | | |
| 10.00 | | | | |
| 10.20 | | | | |
| 10.30 | Disposal of unused cuttings for various other uses, including SDI | | Typing summaries at word processor | Numbering summaries and cuttings, then filing cuttings |
| 11.00 | Checking bulletin text at the word processor | | Checking bulletin processing at the word processor | |
| 11.30 | | | Printing master copy of bulletin at the word processor and making early photocopies | |
| 11.45 | | | | Taking master copy of bulletin to printing |
| 12.00 | | | | Adding new items to the 'cut and stick' index |
| 12.45 | | | | |
| 1.00 | | | | |
| 2.00 | | | | On its return from printing, addressing bulletin |
| 2.30 | | | | |

\* Several clerical officers share DIB tasks and it is unusual for the same officer to perform all the day's tasks

NB Information Officers often encounter a 'slack' period after they have scanned and selected and before the editor has decided which cuttings are to be used.

**Figure 2. Chart of the DIB production process before computerisation**

52

at the Library, at about 8.45 a.m., Information Officers complete their scanning and selection and pass their cuttings to one of their number who is acting as editor. There is a rota so that three or four Information Officers take regular turns to be the editor. (Each Information Officer is a subject specialist for the purposes of the other Research Library duties which he or she performs. Since DIB is supposed to cover the full range of topics dealt with by the Library, it is thought preferable to 'rotate' the editors so as to reduce the risk of undue emphasis in one particular topic.) There are nearly always too many cuttings for the limited space available in the bulletin. DIB is never more than one sheet because (1) a two-sheet bulletin would have to be stapled, which would cause delay; (2) a stapled bulletin would increase the risk of jamming our addressing machine; (3) most important, we believe that more than one sheet daily would probably not be read. Many of our users are hard-pressed councillors and senior officers with plenty of other material to read. Therefore the editor now rejects some cuttings, using the DIB indexes to check any stories which he or she believes may have been reported before from another source. Any press notices which have arrived since the previous issue of the bulletin are also checked. Then the editor hands the surviving cuttings (and press notices) back to the other Information Officers. They write the summaries and source citations by hand on slips of paper. In order to save space and time, there are standard abbreviations for many of the sources – 'G' for *Guardian*, 'T' for *Times* and 'Tel' for *Daily Telegraph*, for instance. The Information Officers also assign subject headings from the standard list. Beneath the subject heading they may sometimes add a (usually geographical) subheading. Having completed this task, and having handed summaries and cuttings back to the editor, the other Information Officers have completed their contribution to today's DIB. It is about 10 a.m.

### Editing – old-style

As completed summaries come in, the editor checks and amends them. Accuracy is very important. Any implication of prejudice on the part of the bulletin, whether by wrong emphasis, or omission, or turn of phrase, must be avoided. Figures must be exact. Councillors' names must be spelt correctly. Subject headings must be as precise as possible, because indexing and retrieval depend upon them. When alterations have been made, the editor sorts the summaries and cuttings into alphabetical subject heading order. Then a clerical assistant gives each summary, along with its related cuttings, a unique DIB item number and takes the cuttings away to be filed. A typist takes the summaries and keys them on to a Wang word processor, which the Research Library has been using since 1979. She also types in the day's date, and the name of the editor. While typing is taking place the editor can dispose of the unused cuttings. Perhaps they will be added to earlier

53

DIB cuttings on the same story which have already been filed – the DIB indexes can be checked to find the correct item numbers. Perhaps subject-specialist Information Officers will send them to individual customers as part of the Library's SDI service. More substantial items may be submitted for the monthly *Urban Abstracts* bulletin. When typing is completed at about 11 a.m. both editor and typist sit at the word processor and make a final check. If the text is too long, some last-minute paring-down is necessary. Some items may be deleted altogether. At about 11.30 a.m. the editor's contribution for the day is complete.

*Filing, printing and dispatch*

Now the day's bulletin is printed, at the Wang daisy wheel printer, on to a sheet of standard *Daily Intelligence Bulletin* headed stationery. A few photocopies are made – for display in the Library, for indexing, and for early distribution to the Leader of the Council and a few other 'VIPs' – and then the master copy is taken to the Council's offset print shop. A clerical assistant now takes one of the photocopies and cuts it into horizontal strips so that each summary, along with its source citation, item number and subject heading, is separate. These are then pasted on to appropriately subject-headed index pages (Figure 3). This 'cut and stick' index takes about half an hour to bring up to date each day. Just after lunch DIB is returned from the print shop and fed through the Library's addressing machine. If the machine operates well, the job will take about half an hour, and the bulletin can be dispatched at between 2 and 3 p.m.

**Producing DIB after computerisation**

During the past two years we have been creating a computerised DIB 'database'. Our database is a collection of machine-readable records, each of which comprises a number of separate pieces of information or 'fields'. The Adlib package has enabled us to (1) put data into the database; (2) select data from within the database; (3) amend data in the database; (4) manipulate the data to create printouts. In our case the records on the database are DIB items, and the fields are DIB number, subject heading, summary and others.

Adlib, like many similar packages, permits considerable flexibility in the way the database is set up. It consists of a set of programs which can be used in different combinations to achieve a wide range of objectives. Consequently, the design of our DIB database was able to follow the specifications already laid down in the printed bulletin. The bought-in package did not dictate the form or content of our bulletin; each record in the database contains the same pieces of information as were already being created.

54

**3418**
Parking—London

The GLC is to take tougher action against diplomats who abuse London's parking laws; diplomats' unpaid parking tickets may no longer be automatically cancelled (DIB 3337). (GLC Press Notice 188 17/6; Tel 19/6 p3)

**3485**
Parking—London

Article discussing the increased incidence of illegal parking on pavements in towns and the remedy being applied by Westminster City Council of photographing the culprits. (G 23/6 p16)

**3705**
Parking—London

Report on the GLC's efforts to persuade foreign diplomats to recognise London's parking restrictions (see also DIB 3337, 3418). (Tel 1/7 p8)

**3706**
Parking—London

Report that Sir Malby Crofton, newly appointed GLC law and order spokesman, has said that he would like to see the "bulldog" wheel clamp introduced for illegally parked cars. (EN (City P) 30/6 p8)

**3707**
Parking—London

Article by Glenys Roberts claiming that the system of residents' parking permits has broken down in Central London, due to inadequate control of the issue of permits and the use of parking bays by non-residents. (EN (Clos P) 30/6 p6)

**3804**
Parking—London

A proposal to introduce "bulldog" clamps to immobilise illegally parked or untaxed vehicles will be considered by the GLC Planning and Communications Policy Committee next week. (EN (Clos P) 3/7 p9: ES (Clos P) p5)

**4051**
Parking—London

Report on the proposals by John Wheeler, MP, for a "tougher but faster" control of parking in central London. (ES (Clos P) 15/7 p8)

**4168**
Parking—London

The GLC's Planning and Communications Policy Committee is urging tougher measures against illegal parking, particularly by diplomats, and may seek responsibility for parking enforcement in London. (DIB 3804) (LT News 18/7 p3)

**4241**
Parking—London

An experimental no parking scheme operative for one hour only in the middle of each weekday may be introduced at Bush Hill Park, Enfield, in an attempt to beat car commuters who park all day in the side streets instead of using the station car park. (Motor Transport 19/7 p15)

**4242**
Parking—London

Shirley Porter, Westminster Council Highways Committee Chairman, has called for London's traffic wardens to be given a new image and awarded greater status. (ES (City P) 24/7 p8)

**4520**
Parking—London

Brief report on continued deadlock in the traffic wardens' pay talks. (EN (City P) 7/8 p8)

**4636**
Parking—London

Report that traffic wardens in London are now so underpaid and short-staffed that their union is recommending that they apply for alternative jobs in the civil service. (G 14/8 p3)

Do not stick items below this line

**Figure 3. DIB Subject Heading Page**

In the following description of how DIB is now produced we try to give details of some of the features of the new system. Let us wind the clock back to 1984 (Figure 4). It is 8.45 a.m. and the Information Officers have just arrived with their newspapers. The scene in the DIB room has changed considerably. Space has been made for three CIFER 2634 visual display terminals. So far, though, we cannot see what effect computerisation has had on DIB production. The Information Officers pass their cuttings to the editor, who sifts through, as usual, to decide today's selection. Now, however, when the editor comes to check whether a particular story has been included before, he or she turns to one of the terminals and conducts on-line searches on the DIB database. The editor then passes the chosen cuttings back to the Information Officers. Two of them use the other two terminals in the room. The rest go to terminals in other parts of the Library — terminals which later in the day are used for various aspects of housekeeping (book ordering, cataloguing and the loans system).

Each Information Officer calls up a specially formatted blank DIB screen at his or her terminal and keys summaries, citations and subject headings into specified places or 'fields' on the screen. Text can only be keyed into these fields, and not elsewhere on the screen. These fields, the edges of which are denoted by brackets, have been defined by us, and the terminal will not allow any data to be inserted in the 'protected' parts of the screen (i.e. those parts which are not within fields). This formatting enables the programs to discern which data belongs in which field of each record. The DIB number, for instance, will always start at a fixed number of lines down the screen and at a fixed number of characters from the left. This precision, through positioning on the screen, in distinguishing one field from another, is essential to the indexing process, as will be explained below. (A typical DIB screen, with an item typed into it, is shown in Appendix 1.) The four or five Information Officers key items in simultaneously. Often the editor also undertakes some keying-in. As soon as an item has been completed, the Information Officer sends it to the DIB database, on which all previous items since 1982 are stored, and calls up a new blank DIB screen. As each new item is begun, a special program automatically allocates a unique consecutive item number. Subject headings cannot be inadvertently invented or mis-spelt because the program checks subject headings against a standard list and will not permit any deviations. (The list can of course be altered when the need arises.) The subheadings, however, are not restricted in this way, and may be added at will. The text of the summary can be keyed in without regard to line-ends. If words are broken between the end of one line and the beginning of the next, the program automatically restores them before they are added to the database and before they are typed out in the bulletin itself. The program checks any newspaper title abbreviations ('T', 'G', etc.) against a standard list, and rejects

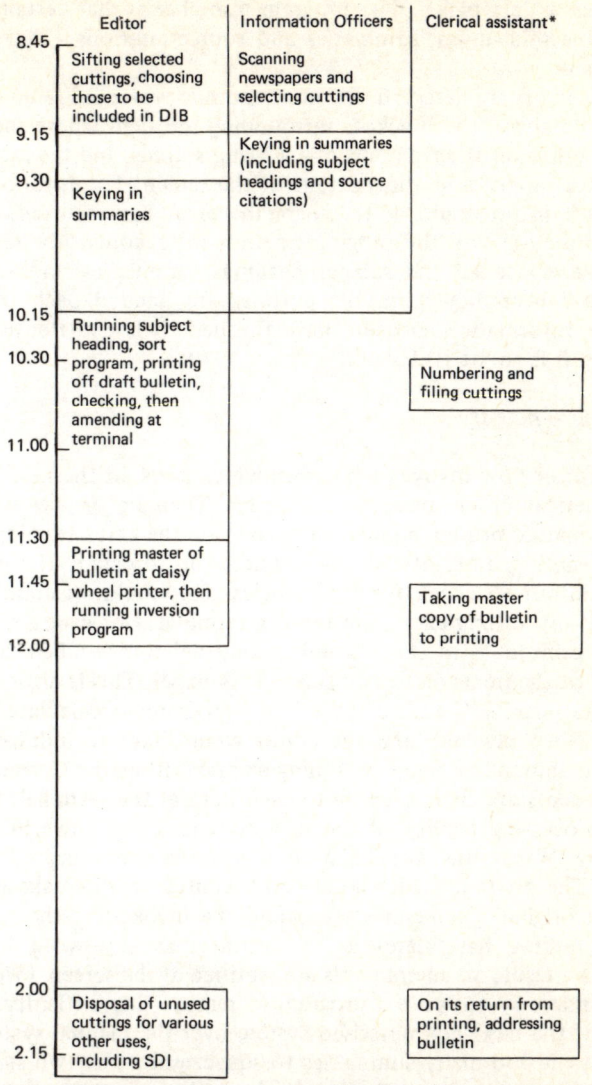

|  | Editor | Information Officers | Clerical assistant* |
|---|---|---|---|
| 8.45 | Sifting selected cuttings, choosing those to be included in DIB | Scanning newspapers and selecting cuttings | |
| 9.15 | | Keying in summaries (including subject headings and source citations) | |
| 9.30 | Keying in summaries | | |
| 10.15 | Running subject heading, sort program, printing off draft bulletin, checking, then amending at terminal | | |
| 10.30 | | | Numbering and filing cuttings |
| 11.00 | | | |
| 11.30 | Printing master of bulletin at daisy wheel printer, then running inversion program | | |
| 11.45 | | | Taking master copy of bulletin to printing |
| 12.00 | | | |
| 2.00 | Disposal of unused cuttings for various other uses, including SDI | | On its return from printing, addressing bulletin |
| 2.15 | | | |

\* Several clerical officers share DIB tasks and it is unusual for the same officer to perform all the day's tasks

NB Information Officers often encounter a 'slack' period after they have scanned and selected and before the editor has decided which cuttings are to be used.

**Figure 4. Chart of the DIB production process after computerisation**

deviations. When the date of the source being cited is the same as the date on which the bulletin is being produced, it need not be keyed in. The program will automatically supply the current date when that part of the screen is left blank. The program also checks that certain key fields — subject headings, summaries and source citations — have not been left blank.

If any errors are detected, the new record is prevented from being sent to the database, the brackets surrounding the field where there is an error or omission flash on and off, a bleep sounds, and the message 'field in error' appears at the bottom of the screen. The Information Officer is left in no doubt as to where the error has occurred! Only upon its correction will the programs permit the record to be sent to the database. Once all the subject headings, summaries and source citations have been keyed in, the cuttings are handed back to the editor. The Information Officers have finished their contribution to today's DIB. It is about 10.15 a.m.

*Editing — new-style*

The editor now invokes a program which sorts all the new items into alphabetical order by subject heading. Then he or she uses an Epson dot matrix printer connected to one of the Cifer terminals to print the resulting draft of the day's bulletin on to paper. The editor uses the printout to check for inaccuracies. This could, of course, be done merely by calling each item up at a terminal. However a second use for the printout is to check whether some deletion will be required in order to fit the items on to two sides of A4 paper. This is difficult to check at the terminal because there is no program to calculate total numbers of lines covered, and the editor would have to indulge in a considerable amount of time-consuming mental arithmetic. Corrections and amendments are then keyed into each item at the terminal. Since the word processing facility of the new system is less powerful than that of the Wang this particular task is more complicated than previously. The program which so cleverly rectifies word breaks at line ends at the original keying-in stage cannot be invoked at the editing stage. The editor has therefore to ensure that any word breaks occurring as a result of amendments are rectified at the screen. (Work is currently underway to write a program to remove this difficulty.) An advantage of the new, computerised system over the manual system is that if there are too many summaries to squeeze into the two sides of the bulletin they need not be deleted. The editor can retain them for the database while omitting them from the bulletin. With all amendments made, the editor goes to a daisy wheel printer terminal connected to the Prime minicomputer and prints the final version of the bulletin on to standard *Daily Intelligence Bulletin* headed stationery. The final version of the bulletin looks very little different from its 1982 predecessor. The editor's last DIB task of the morning is to run an 'inversion' program, which creates and maintains machine-readable indexes to the contents of the database. However, the editor's task for the day is not quite complete because there has not been time to dispose of unused cuttings. This now usually takes place in the early afternoon. The time is now midday.

### Filing and printing

Photocopies for early distribution and for display in the Library are made, and then the master copy is taken to the print shop. A clerical assistant files the cuttings in number order, but no clerical help is needed to prepare the index, because there are now two computerised retrieval facilities — on-line searching of the database, and paper printouts sorted alphabetically by subject heading.

### Dispatch — computerised addressing

The bulletin returns from the print shop, as it always did, shortly after lunch, and is ready to be addressed. Now, however, a new computer-linked addressing system is in use. The piles of inky addressing machine stencils (a separate set for each of the Library's five or six different bulletins, and each having to be changed whenever a recipient moved from one office or building to another) have gone. With the Adlib library housekeeping package we have created a file of borrower records, including name and address. This is primarily for the library loans system. However, we have inserted into each borrower record a field in which is recorded a note of any current awareness bulletins which the borrower wishes to receive, and of how many copies he or she requires (Figure 5). We have written programs which search the borrower records file and retrieve names and addresses of borrowers wishing to receive each bulletin. The programs also sort the retrieved records into departmental order to make mailing more efficient. This retrieval process takes up a considerable amount of computer time and is therefore undertaken only weekly. It is carried out each Monday, and the retrieved records are transferred to a floppy disc which is attached to a Cifer 2684 microcomputer terminal. This device, again using a program which we have written, drives an Addressograph 'Whiz' addressing machine. The appropriate instruction at the microcomputer terminal prompts the addressing machine to address DIB only to those users whose borrower records contain a request for DIB in the bulletins field. Other bulletins are addressed similarly. The programs have been so prepared that the microcomputer terminal can be used simultaneously for other work. The entire process of addressing 1,000 copies of DIB (the other 100 are distributed unaddressed to GLC councillors) now takes 16 minutes — about half the time it used to take on a good day. Furthermore, the borrower/addressee records are more reliable because amendments need only be made to one centralised record rather than to up to six or seven separate stencils as previously. Fast and accurate addressing is a prerequisite of daily current awareness services, and the innovations which we have made in this respect are just as important as those in the bulletin production process itself.

---

KEY (Smith                                                                                              )

— — — — —BORROWER RECORDS— — — — GLC Research Library — — — —

Borrower No: (12345)          Loan Limit : (15)          Items          1    On Loan

Name:        (Smith J                           )          Dept:   (DG)

Address:     (DG/I/IS                            )
             (Room 513                           )
             (                                   )
             (                                   )

Telephone:   (7530                               )

Bulletins:   DIB     BIN     UA1     UA2     TN      ED      P + E
             (03)    (01)    (01)    ( )     ( )     (01)    ( )

---

NB    This user has requested three copies of each issue of DIB, along with
      single copies of each issue of several other bulletins. These will
      automatically be addressed to the user at the location given.

**Figure 5. A record from the 'borrower' file**

### The effect of computerisation on bulletin production

I have explained that DIB is not merely a current awareness bulletin but also a substantial cuttings collection and index, and that retrieval problems were an important factor in the decision to computerise. Could it be said that the advantages of a computerised production system are such that one could justify introducing it for a current awareness bulletin alone?

Solely from the point of view of current awareness the advantages are these:

(1) The numbering and alphabetical sorting of the DIB summaries, formerly undertaken by a clerical officer and the editor respectively, are now both performed by the computer. Note, however, that the numbering of the cuttings before they are filed is still a task requiring clerical time.

(2) The bulletin is now keyed directly by the Information Officers. Formerly a typist typed all of it on to the word processor from hand-written slips. Each summary is therefore written only once.

(3) The editor can be more confident that stories have not been covered before, because she has free text on-line search facilities for the whole

of the text of previous issues, rather than manual index access by subject headings only. A concomitance of this is that the argument for a rota system of editing is strengthened — previously the frequent change of editorship jeopardised continuity of coverage.

(4) Since DIB is now machine-readable, an on-line current awareness service, both to the remoter parts of the GLC and to the London borough town halls, as well as to organisations outside London local government, is feasible. This can of course be combined with an on-line retrieval service from the whole database. These developments are described below.

From the point of view of current awareness, the disadvantages are these:

(1) Although we have cut out several essentially clerical tasks we have not gained time overall. As Figure 6 shows, we have cut drastically the amount of clerical time taken, but more professional time is now required and so the total time taken is nearly the same. The bulletin is issued and distributed at about the same time of day as before computerisation. How have clerical time savings been offset by losses in other parts of the process? First, many of our Information Officers are not trained keyboard operators or typists. Somewhat late in the day we are considering whether to rectify this. Second, the need to type specific parts of each DIB item into specific fields (i.e. subject heading, summary, cited source, etc.) has slowed down the keying-in process. Third, the word processing capabilities of the Adlib package are limited. This slows down later checking and amendment undertaken by the editor. Note, too, that keying-in and checking also take longer because information retrieval considerations demand more care in choice of vocabulary (see below). Fourth, a local problem is that the Prime minicomputer is not reserved for the exclusive use of the Library. It is operated by the GLC's computing department and is shared with several other GLC departments. This means that when use of the computer is heavy, response times are increased, and on-line checking and amendment can be frustratingly slow. On many occasions there can be little doubt that the process of handwriting the summaries and then typing and amending them on the Wang word processor is faster than use of the Adlib package. In extreme cases there have been complete breakdowns of computer service — sometimes because of errors by the computer operators, and sometimes because of repairs or maintenance to the computer itself.

(2) The editor's job has become more complicated. The checklist of tasks she must complete now includes some new, Adlib-related duties. Before any summaries can be entered at the terminals she must check that the Prime computer operator has remembered to enter today's date into the computer itself. Otherwise, not only will the date printed on the DIB be wrong, but the Adlib programs will not add the

Staff time required each day to produce the *Daily Intelligence Bulletin* before and after computerisation

(1) Pre-computerisation:

| Editor | Information Officers (assuming 4) | Typist | Clerical Officers |
|---|---|---|---|
| 2 hr. 45 min. | 5 hr. | 1 hr. 15 min. | 2 hr. 10 min. |
| Total professional: | 7 hr. 45 min. | Total clerical: | 3 hr. 25 min. |

Total time pre-computerisation — 11 hr. 10 min.

(2) Post-computerisation:

| Editor | Information Officers (assuming 4) | Typist | Clerical Officers |
|---|---|---|---|
| 4 hr. | 6 hr. | — | 1 hr. |
| Total professional: | 10 hr. | Total clerical: | 1 hr. |

Total time post-computerisation — 11 hr.

*Notes:*

(1) These are very rough estimates, and include no allowance for staff time in the printing department.

(2) Post-computerisation about 15 minutes of professional staff time is taken up each day in transmitting new data to Scicon. This has not been accounted for since it is not, strictly, part of bulletin production.

(3) Computer systems do 'crash' from time to time, and occasionally several extra hours of professional staff time in trouble-shooting is added to the post-computerisation total.

**Figure 6. Staff time required each day to produce the *Daily Intelligence Bulletin* before and after computerisation.**

new data to the database. In addition the Adlib inversion programs must be invoked so that the indexes can be updated. Neither of these jobs individually takes very long if the programs and the computer are working normally. Collectively though, they are an added burden.

(3) A multi-subject current awareness bulletin prepared by a team of Information Officers, who for the rest of their work time are largely subject-specialists, relies for efficient selection of stories on communication between the compilers at the time of compilation.

Computerisation has reduced the opportunities for such communication because, since there are not enough terminals in the DIB room, some Information Officers are obliged to write in isolation at terminals in other parts of the Library. This is of course a local accommodation problem rather than one which arises directly from computerisation itself.

### Effect of computerisation on retrieval problems

In some respects, then, we have made the current awareness task more difficult and slower in exchange for a great improvement in indexing and retrieval. The 'cut and stick' manual indexes (Figure 3) have two flaws. First, they allow access only by subject heading. Words or phrases in the summaries themselves are not searchable, nor are the source citations. Second, they are annual indexes and are not cumulative. A search through the manual indexes is a daunting and not always rewarding task. A given topic may appear under several different headings because of the differing decisions of editors over the years, and because of variations in emphasis in the reports themselves.

#### *Index creation (inversion)*

The use of Adlib has made retrieval easier and more efficient. Whereas previously only subject headings were searchable, now words in the summaries and source citations, and dates may be retrieved as well. Since November 1982 each day's DIB items have been added to the database. In addition, all the DIB items written between 1 January 1982 and November 1982 have been added retrospectively to the database, having been converted from paper to machine-readable form using optical character recognition (OCR) techniques. Remarkable as optical character recognition is, there remain some complications in its use. The process of converting DIB items from paper to machine-readable form involved more than the mere recognition of letters. The Adlib software requires each section or field of a DIB item to be identified separately so that separate indexes to each field can be created. It is simple for the human reader to discern from the printed page the subject heading, DIB item number, summary, cited source and so on. It is equally simple to distinguish between one DIB item and the next. These are more difficult processes for the OCR machine, which has to be programmed to detect such distinctions through relative position and length of gaps. Furthermore, we had to take account of words which, in our pre-computerised bulletins, we had split between two lines and hyphenated. Although the OCR work undertaken for us was of a high quality, a considerable amount of manual inspection and adjustment (sometimes through the use of specially written programs) was required before the items could be added to the database.

All records added to the database have been inverted in order to create machine-readable indexes. There are several indexes.

There is an index of words and phrases which are approved subject headings. This was originally used to print out a weekly paper index which took the same form as the old 'cut and stick' index. The paper index was intended for use by customers not wishing to learn how to search on-line, and was also seen as a back-up, should the computerised searching facility be temporarily unavailable for any reason. We have now abandoned the weekly re-run of this paper version of the index because it uses a great deal of computer time and, with its increasing size, has become very cumbersome to use. The on-line facility has almost always been available, and users have much preferred to ask Research Library staff to run printouts from on-line searches for them than to use the paper copy indexes!

There is a 'free text' index of words in the subject headings and/or the summaries field and of abbreviations in the source citations field.

There are also indexes of newspaper title abbreviations, DIB dates, and publication dates of sources cited.

For each word, phrase or abbreviation in an index there is a record of the DIB numbers of the DIB items in which that word, phrase or abbreviation occurs and a record of physical location of those items on the computer disc. Each day's DIB items are analysed by an inversion program. Where words, phrases or abbreviations found by the inversion program have occurred in earlier DIB items the new item numbers and disc locations are added to the existing index entries. Where new ones occur, new index entries are created. Certain 'stop words', such as conjunctions, the definite and indefinite articles, and prepositions, are deliberately omitted from the indexes because they are of no use for retrieval purposes and because their inclusion would slow down the inversion process and waste computer time and space. Inversion speeds up on-line retrieval because it is much quicker for the computer to check machine-readable indexes than to search the entire text of all the DIB items stored in the database for the occurrences of a required word or phrase.

### Searching the DIB database

Although the DIB database created using Adlib can be searched on-line we cannot use complete Boolean logic search statements. A search has to be done in stages, first by selecting a set from the database by the use of one search term, then 'refining' the results of this search by the use of other terms. An example of a search is given in full in Appendix 2.

The result of such a search can be merely the display of the retrieved items at the terminal, or a printout of all the items retrieved in the same format as that in which they appear in the bulletin. Such printouts, which we call 'Diblists', may be sorted into date, reverse date, or subject heading order (Figure 7).

## 'EQUAL OPPORTUNITIES POLICIES'

**8202141**
**Race relations**

The CRE recommends an equal opportunities policy for local authorities in their report published yesterday: 'Local Government and Racial Equality'. (G 29/4 p4: T p2)

**8205177**
**Equal**
**opportunities**

Islington Council is to 'classify' its employees according to racial background and sex as part of its policy to equal opportunity and employment. (Tel 09/10 p6)

**8205542**
**Equal**
**opportunities**
**Islington**

Letter from Islington Council chief executive H M Dewing explaining the Council's policies on equal opportunities and ethnic record-keeping. (Tel 28/10 p18)

**8205906**
**Equal**
**opportunities**

The Equal Pay Act will be amended this session following Britain's infringement under Common Market legislation and its failure to provide a proper equal pay framework. Also an article by John Carr, GLC Staff Committee Chair on Labour Councils' implementations of equal opportunities policies. (DE PN 11/11: Tribune 12/11 p2)

**8307536**
**Equal**
**opportunities**

ILEA is to convene a special caucus of women members to ensure that the views of women's organisations and individuals are considered in formulating equal opportunities policy. (ILEA PN 83/15 15/02)

**8307939**
**Equal**
**opportunities**

The TUC yesterday published a report, 'Women in the Labour Market', which concludes that unemployment, new technology and Government policies have led to 'an appalling waste of women's skills and experience'. (FT 09/03 p11: G p4)

**8308144**
**Equal**
**opportunities**

The TUC women's conference yesterday launched a campaign to win full equality of employment opportunity and rejected the findings of the Government's family policy group. (T 18/03 p2)

**8310700**
**Equal**
**opportunities**

Islington Council's equal opportunities employment policy statement says that homosexuals may be recruited to any council job. (S (City P) 29/07 p2: Tel 30/07 p2)

**8311139**
**Equal**
**opportunities**

'Implementing Equal Employment Opportunity Policies' published yesterday by the CRE states that more employers are using positive discrimination techniques under the Race Relations Act 1976 to achieve equality of opportunity. (S 24/08 p2: FT p8)

**8311368**
**Equal**
**opportunities**
**Islington**

Islington Council, as part of its equal opportunities policy, is to give the right to appeal to applicants who fail to get jobs with the Council. (Tel 03/09 p5)

**8311409**
**Equal**
**opportunities**

Very brief report that Camden Council plans to recruit female refuse collectors and drivers as part of its equal opportunities policy. (Tel 06/09 p13)

**8311713**
**Equal**
**opportunities**

As part of its equal opportunities policy 'to stamp out racism' Islington Council is to ask the ethnic origin of applicants for parking permits, rent rebates, meals on wheels and library membership. (Tel 21/09 p12)

**8311873**
**Equal**
**opportunities**
**Islington**

Islington Council is to ask the ethnic origin of people applying for rates and rent rebates, meals-on-wheels, library membership and parking permits as part of its equal opportunities policy. (S (City P) 28/09 p12)

**8312718**
**Equal**
**opportunities**

Article by Brenda Emmanus which looks at the GLC's equal opportunities policy, its work for ethnic minority communities and the implications of the proposed abolition of the GLC. (The Voice 15/11 p14,15)

**Figure 7. DIB list printout**

## Effect of information retrieval considerations on the contents of the bulletin

We have said that computerisation has not affected the contents of the bulletin. As regards its information content, this is true. However, computerisation has brought the possibility of greatly improved information retrieval, and in order to realise that possibility to the maximum we have had to make alterations. Efficient retrieval requires consistency in the use of vocabulary. Whereas previously only subject headings needed to be consistent for retrieval purposes, now summary and citation must also conform. Much of the resulting standardisation is in the form of abbreviations, which have always been favoured in any case because of shortage of space in the bulletin, but which are now more strictly adhered to. It is always 'RSG' and not 'rate support grant', for example. Similarly, it is 'DOE' and not 'Department of the Environment', and 'Local Govt Chron', not 'Local Government Chronicle'. Another example of the consistency which retrieval considerations have imposed is in the form of personal names. It is now always 'Patrick Jenkin', for instance, rather than 'Mr Jenkin', so that, in retrieval, there will be no confusion between this and any other man with the same surname. When possible, in order to increase the chances of retrieval, synonyms for the words used in subject headings are used in the summaries.

There is a conflict between the urgency of current awareness and the meticulous accuracy of a properly indexed retrieval system, and the degree to which each of these two needs should be accommodated remains unsolved.

## Achieving wider use of the DIB database

The DIB database as mounted on the Prime 750 minicomputer, and using the Adlib programs for searching and retrieval is a major advance on what was available only two years ago. However full Boolean logic searching is not available and, more important, access to the Prime 750 is restricted to a very few users because its capacity is relatively small. If wider usage of the database is to be achieved, it is necessary to transfer it to the GLC's IBM 3083 mainframe computer. The mainframe is accessible, either by direct cable link or by dialling up, from about 500 GLC terminals and from many London borough council terminals. We have therefore copied the DIB database to the mainframe, where it is handled using the IBM STAIRS package. We also copy across daily updates. Not only does this offer far wider access, but full Boolean logic searching is possible. DIB continues to be compiled and indexed using Adlib and our own programs on the Prime 750 (these cannot all be done using STAIRS), but searching is now increasingly carried out using STAIRS. In the STAIRS version DIB is coupled with another Research Library current awareness bulletin,

*Tech News* (a weekly bulletin for architects, engineers and environmental scientists which is also created using Adlib), and the combined database is known as 'Urbaline'. Many GLC and London borough officers are already using Urbaline at their own terminals.

### On-line current awareness

Since the version of Urbaline which is mounted on the mainframe computer is updated daily, we can now offer on-line current awareness services. By early afternoon users can access the new items, either for reading at their terminals or for printing off and for local circulation. Alternatively users can merely retrieve items on their own special subjects. Since STAIRS also allows searches to be saved and then reinvoked at will, users can also compile and run their own SDI profiles in conjuction with the Urbaline service. This muddies the waters as far as the conflict between current awareness and information retrieval is concerned, because, whereas vocabulary control is unimportant for current awareness, it is just as important for SDI as it is for retrospective information retrieval. Urbaline is new, and much training of users remains to be done before the service can become fully effective. It therefore remains to be seen whether it will be a success. Certainly postal and internal delivery delays make the paper bulletin version of DIB somewhat less than 'current' for outlying GLC offices (there are many in various parts of London) and for London borough town halls.

A second on-line retrieval and current awareness service based on DIB and *Tech News* is that offered by Scicon Ltd, one of the commercial host organisations which already offers the Research Library's other on-line database, ACOMPLINE (A COMPuterised London Information NEtwork).

ACOMPLINE is the Research Library's bibliographical database covering books, pamphlets, reports and major journal articles about local government.[4]

New DIB and *Tech News* items are transmitted daily by telephone line from the GLC to Scicon's Milton Keynes computer, using the Library's Cifer 2684 microcomputer terminal. This is a similar arrangement to that used by the House of Commons Library to transmit POLIS data to Scicon. The new items are transmitted as soon as DIB or *Tech News* has been compiled, so that Scicon's subscribers are able to print off the complete current awareness bulletin for their own use by early afternoon. It should be noted that the transmission of data to Scicon takes at least 15 minutes of Library staff time each day — which is in addition to the time charted in Figure 4.

A brief summary of some of the ways in which users outside London local government can make use of Urbaline has been published.[3]

GLC councillors and officers can call on the Research Library for a 'back-up' photocopy service and we have seen that demand is high. Will the ability which on-line brings to access new DIB items more quickly lead to greater demand for such back-up? What about those Urbaline users to whom the Research Library does not offer photocopy services, the London borough town halls and Scicon's customers? Where an alternative library service is not already offered, will potential Urbaline users be prepared to help themselves? A redeeming factor for Urbaline is that it covers a relatively few, easily accessible newspapers and it would not require very many extra resources or effort to provide local back-up. However, one non-London local government librarian has told us that, while she will use the service for retrospective searching, she will not use it as a current awareness service because she would thereby become less 'aware' herself. In her case scanning for current awareness services helps her to do the rest of her job (enquiries, stock selection and SDI) more effectively. For those organisations not employing a librarian or information specialist the picture may be different. There, perhaps, they may be prepared to use on-line current awareness and to use existing clerical staff to provide the back-up.

## Summary and conclusions

*The case for computerisation of current awareness alone not proven . . .*

In just over two years we have converted a manually produced current awareness bulletin into a fully computerised system offering, in addition to the original paper bulletin, widely available on-line current awareness, SDI and information retrieval. The system has, very largely, exploited resources which are shared either with other functions of the library or with other departments of the GLC. This makes costing of the DIB conversion alone very nearly impossible. The licence to use the Adlib package costs about £12,000 per year – but the Library's circulation, ordering and cataloguing systems all benefit. Similarly, each Cifer 2634 terminal costs about £1,200 – but they are also used for all other Adlib applications and for on-line searching of external databases. The Addressograph Whiz printer cost about £6,000 but is used not only for all Research Library mailing but also by other GLC departments. A Prime 750 minicomputer costs at least £120,000. Needless to say, the one we use has very many other non-Library functions! A large amount of staff time has been invested in development and training. A rough estimate is that two person-years were spent on this, given that one professional member of staff from the Research Library and another from the Methodology Group have been working on the Adlib project as a whole quite intensively since early 1982. Furthermore, about the same staff time as before is required for day-to-day production of the bulletin.

### ... but general library services have benefited

We have described how, for the DIB editors and writers, computerisation has created an as yet unresolved conflict (as to how summaries are to be written and how vocabulary is to be used), between the interests of current awareness and those of information retrieval. In terms of choice of stories too, a conflict between current awareness and information retrieval has emerged. Should we include stories which are of immediate but possibly not long-term interest? However, unresolved as the conflict may be for the compilers, the usage of the Urbaline database for information retrieval by the Research Library staff as a whole is rising steadily. By autumn 1984 16 per cent of all enquiries taken were answered wholly or in part by using Urbaline. This compares with about 10 per cent 12 months previously, and the trend is still upwards. The DIB current awareness bulletin, once rather separate from other Research Library services, is now an integral part of those services. While the benefits of computerisation for the current awareness bulletin remain unproven, its success as an information retrieval tool is undeniable.

### Notes

1. Golland, R., 'The Greater London Council Research Library – computerised information services for local government', *Planning and Administration*, 1984, vol. 11, no. 2, 43–53.
2. 'The GLC Research Library's adoption of Adlib', *Vine*, 1983, vol. 50, 14–21.
3. Golland, R., 'Housing information on Urbaline', *ASSIGnation*, 1984, vol. 2, no. 1, 14–16.
4. Farmer, P. and Gomersall, A., 'ACOMPLINE – an on-line information system for local government', *Journal of Information Science*, 1981, vol. 3, no. 6, 289–94.

## Appendix 1

### A typical DIB screen, with a DIB item typed into it:

---

|  |  |  | DIB No 8406551 |
|---|---|---|---|

Term (Housing                    )              DIB Date            (16/10/84)
     (Newham                     )
Text (Comment on the issues raised by the recent controversy over the Ronan)
     (Point tower blocks with estimates of the extent of defects in similar UK)
     (high rise housing.                                                      )
     (                                                                        )
     (                                                                        )
     (                                                                        )

Notes (                                                                       )
      (                                                                       )

| Source (Abbr) | Publctn Date | Pages | Edition | Source (In Full) |
|---|---|---|---|---|
| (        ) | (12/10/84) | (        ) | (        ) | (AMA PN 169/84        ) |
| (Tel     ) | (16/10/84) | (10       ) | (        ) | (                     ) |
| (        ) | (        ) | (        ) | (        ) | (                     ) |
| (        ) | (        ) | (        ) | (        ) | (                     ) |
| (        ) | (        ) | (        ) | (        ) | (                     ) |
| (        ) | (        ) | (        ) | (        ) | (                     ) |

---

Notes on the fields:

(1) 'DIB No' is the unique item number allocated to this record.

(2) 'Term' is the subject heading ('housing'), along with, in this case, a subheading ('Newham') which, when included, must be entered on the second line of the field.

(3) 'DIB Date' is the date of input of the record to the database. This date is entered automatically by the programs, which use the date keyed in by the Prime operator when the computer is switched on each day. This date is printed out automatically at the top of the front page of the bulletin (see Figure 1).

(4) 'Text' is the Information Officer's summary.

(5) 'Notes' is a field into which messages may be placed. For example: 'This item is too long to be photocopied but is available for reference in the Research Library'. The 'Notes' field is separate from the 'Text' field because, when the inversion programs create an index to the contents of that field we do not want messages such as these to be included. They will be printed out in the bulletin and stored on the database, but will not be searchable.

(6) 'Source (Abbr)' is the field into which newspaper title abbreviations such as G, T or Tel may be put. This field is one of those in which the programs check the contents against a standard list. If any non-standard

abbreviation is included it will be rejected. The standard list against which checks are made contains abbreviations only of those newspapers used most frequently. We have thought it unnecessary to include abbreviations of all possible sources because many are used very little.

(7) 'Publctn date' indicates date of issue of the newspaper, journal or press cutting being cited, and is not necessarily the same as the DIB date.

(8) 'Pages' indicates the page number(s) of the newspaper or journal being cited.

(9) 'Edition' indicates when necessary the specific edition of the newspaper being cited.

(10) 'Source (In Full)'. When the title of a newspaper, journal or press notice issuing body is not on the standard list (see Note 6) it may be entered here. In the example given, an Association of Metropolitan Authorities (AMA) press notice is cited.

The same DIB item, when printed out in the bulletin looks like this:

---

84  06551

Housing   Comment on the issues raised by the recent controversy over
Newham   the Ronan Point tower blocks with estimates of the extent
of defects in similar UK high rise housing.
(AMA PN 169/84 12/10;   Tel 16/10 p10)

---

Where an item has been found in more than one source, the sources cited have been sorted into date order, and sources of different dates separated by a semi-colon. A 'p' has been added to indicate page. When several sources from the same date are cited they are sorted alphabetically.

## Appendix 2

### Example of on-line search of the DIB database

Let us suppose that we have been asked to find all items about asbestos which have been published in the *Guardian* since 1 Sept 1984.

| Message from computer | User's reply | Notes |
|---|---|---|
| TASK: | *SE* | User orders a search of the database. |
| SELECT IF: | *ANY USES ASBESTOS*: | User orders selection of all records in the database which contain the word 'asbestos'. |
| COMMENCING SELECTION | | Instruction acknowledged and being carried out. |
| TOTAL OF 220 MATCHING RECORDS | | There are 220 DIB items in the database containing the word 'asbestos'. |
| REFINE?: | *YES* | User chooses to refine the search – i.e. to use another criterion. |
| SELECT IF: | *SOURCABB=G*: | Criterion specified is that the records should contain citations from the *Guardian*. |
| COMMENCING SELECTION | | Instruction acknowledged and being carried out. |
| TOTAL OF 37 MATCHING RECORDS | | There are 37 DIB items in the database which contain the word 'asbestos' and citation from the *Guardian*. |
| REFINE?: | *YES* | User chooses to refine the search again. |

| Message from computer | User's reply | Notes |
|---|---|---|
| SELECT IF: | *DIBDATE>01/09/84*: | Criterion specified is that the records should be dated 1 September 1984 or later. |
| COMMENCING SELECTION | | Instruction acknowledged and being carried out. |
| TOTAL OF 2 MATCHING RECORDS | | There are 2 DIB items in the database which contain the word 'asbestos', contain citation from the *Guardian*, and are dated 1 September or later. |
| REFINE?: | *NO* | User decides not to refine the search further. |
| TASK: | *MD* | User orders a display of the retrieved items. |

# 6               Present-day developments in current awareness services

*Jane Rogers*

This is the report of a survey carried out among industrial information units in the summer of 1985. The aim was to discover how current awareness service and attitudes to its provision had developed in response to the impact of computers and communication technology, to the greater accessibility of secondary bibliographic sources, and the problems and opportunities seen by management. Also how did attitudes and techniques in 1985 match up to the classical aims of current awareness service, and did the services of the present (and those planned for the future) represent an improvement on the past?

A current awareness service aims to keep the customers of an information service informed about what has been said and written in the current literature that corresponds to their own subject interests. In its traditional form the service consists of scanning the current literature for items of relevance to customers and notifying them immediately, either by personal notification, or through a current awareness bulletin. The theory is that the information unit is doing for the user what he is unable to do for himself — either through lack of time or lack of inclination.

A professional needs to keep him or herself currently informed about what is happening within his field. While this is essential for the well-being of project work, it is also a very time-consuming process. The information unit makes up for the lack of regular contact with the literature by providing a comprehensive current awareness service. Their contribution is to ensure that relevant facts and ideas are brought to the attention of a professional, regardless of the amount of scanning he is prepared to do. The information worker, as it were, looks over the shoulder of the professional he serves, and reads the current literature with the client's present and future possible needs in mind.

When examining provision for current awareness it is important to see it from three different points of view. First, benefit should be derived — benefit to individual users and benefit to the organisation itself. The user benefits by having part of his literature scanning done for him, but also because useful inputs to his or her work are found. Second, a service has to be cost-efficient, so that statements can be made about the large number of clients that can be served at a cost of $x$ pounds, or that the unit cost of the bulletin is low in comparison with similar organisations elsewhere. Third, an effective service has to be supplied, since otherwise the customers will not want to use it.

For example, it must cover the publications where relevant material might be found, and inform the customer of something new before the customer has seen it himself. The information worker must be able to recognise what is relevant, and pass on notifications which are sufficiently informative to stimulate the customer to obtain the material and look at it.

It is not enough for an information unit to supply a current awareness service. The service has to be worthwhile to the users and seen to be worthwhile, in terms of financial outlay, by senior management. This means that the information manager has the job of balancing concern about cost-efficiency from senior management with the needs of his users for effectiveness and benefit.

### The influence of the past

For many years libraries and information services in industry have operated current awareness services of one form or another. A healthy debate has always taken place, with views expressed for or against the different approaches to current awareness services which have been available at any one time. There is no denying the influence of external events on the development of current awareness service in the past. Presumably the techniques and attitudes which are reported in the literature of current awareness service are a contributing factor to the sort of current awareness service given today. They are also of interest because from an examination of what has gone before it can be seen whether the present forms of current awareness, operating in the so-called 'age of new technology', are really advances on the old.

Luhn's article 'A business intelligence system' published in 1958 in the *IBM Journal of Research and Development*, and a subsequent article in *American Documentation*, represent something of a milestone in current awareness service. Luhn described, among other things, the use of computers to prepare rotated title indexes to new publications, which would then be sent to professional people to keep them informed. However, as East points out, mechanisation of information services proceeded more slowly in the UK than in the States because the relative cheapness and availability of human effort in the 1950s did not help create great incentives towards mechanisation. Also the UK had fewer large organisations in which costly computerised systems could be developed. Lastly, well developed conventional information systems already existed in many industrial situations.

A different approach, also described by Luhn, in which users' requirements in the form of word 'profiles' were matched against document input in the form of references to journal articles and reports, was introduced at the UK Atomic Energy Authority's Culham Laboratory (Anthony et al. 1968). The computer was seen here as extending the coverage of the current awareness service without the information unit's having to look through new material, meeting the demands of more users for a personal notification service, and coping with the growing volume of literature.

In the early 1960s the reasons given by East (cheap labour and the absence of large organisations able to support computerisation) delayed the effect of computers on information work. However, at this time two other initiatives began to have an impact. First, machine-readable databases became available as a byproduct of the compilation of secondary services (abstracting and indexing services to the primary literature), and tapes of these could be leased from the database producers. Second, a Chemical Society research unit at the University of Nottingham began running magnetic tapes from Chemical Abstracts Services against search profiles in a free trial of 'computer SDI' to selected information services, for distribution to their clients. At UKAEA Harwell in-house computer SDI from Nuclear Science Abstracts tapes enabled their information service to meet the needs of a larger number of users, but even at that time it was realised that the interests of their clients extended well beyond what the computerised SDI was capable of providing.

It is essential that one appreciates how influential were the early 1970s on the provision of current awareness service. Haygarth Jackson of ICI listed 'the more crucial impact factors', among which were:

> Exponential growth of the literature
> More users of the information service
> Increase in the number of specialised fields of interest
> Need for a multi-disciplinary approach to the literature
> Increase in the speed information is needed
> Increasing cost of staff
> Increasing availability of computers
> Demands for increases in profitability and productivity
> Increasing cost consciousness
> Need to improve the information services

Especially among the larger units, these factors seemed to have resulted in a widespread move towards computer SDI — use of in-house computer services to spin tapes for a centralised SDI service, or the obtaining of batch computer SDI from UKCIS at the University of Nottingham, or from the database producers themselves (INSPEC, ISI, etc.). Dammers of Shell explained that the move to computerised SDI avoided labour-intensive manual techniques, and was necessary anyway because of the rapid expansion of the world's literature. However others felt that the move was dictated solely by economic necessity, with little regard for whether it was the best option. Saunderson of ICI felt that information units were being 'forced into a position of almost total reliance on the secondary services for the provision of current awareness and retrieval services to the published literature'. 'Computerised SDIs supplied from outside are by no means necessarily the final and even the best answer, and it must be acknowledged that much of the pressure to use them has been dictated by financial stringency' (Arnold 1972). A variety of opinion was expressed on the use of secondary services for current awareness. By and large these views seem to have been influenced by the circumstances of the holder – principally by the resources available to the information unit.

In defence of computer SDI and against in-house scanning, Dammers seemed the principal proponent. Apart from the arguments relating to labour costs and the growth of the literature, Dammers maintained that the user is the only reliable judge of relevance, and using an intermediary between him and the published literature is a system of doubtful merit. Instead a system where the researcher selects his own literature by his search profile, which he adjusts himself, is preferable. In any case it is 'virtually impossible' to demonstrate the economic merits of an extension to the information budget in order to allow manual scanning to continue. (Dammers worked for a large corporation able to lease tapes of secondary services for centralised searching to produce in-house SDI.)

In defence of manual current awareness services from scanning published material, it was said that in-house scanning is more suitable than the secondary services for a unique audience, whose requirements can be understood and catered for in more depth than references from secondary services can supply. Reliance on secondary services also means that useful items are missed, and the customer is alerted to items much later. Nightingale (1973) and Blick (1975) were able to supply cost-benefit justification of information bulletins which showed that the cost of manual scanning to produce a bulletin was small compared with the total cost of the time its recipients would have to spend in scanning for themselves to obtain the references it contained. Profile construction for a mechanised service has to be careful and thorough, and demands detailed knowledge of database systems on the part of the information provider. Profiles have to be modified in an attempt to improve retrieval, and also keep in line with the constant changes in customers' work and interests, if a useful output is to be obtained. It is difficult to see how the information workers save time by abandoning a manual service, particularly since time and time again observers have shown that, compared with SDI from computerised secondary services, manual scanning performs much better in respect of coverage, timeliness, relevance, selectivity, access to material, and content of notification. 'Current awareness' from secondary services is clearly not relevant to situations where current information is a prerequisite for success.

A third approach to secondary services is one that is aware of their shortcomings but sees them as a supplementary source of references for current awareness service to scanning primary material. For instance at Harwell visual scanning of the primary literature was selected to satisfy the needs of contract R & D for industry, and computer SDI for a service in other areas 'not at the forefront of the service, [but] used for the baseload, leaving human systems to look ahead and anticipate requirements' (Terry and Jones 1972). A common attitude to computer SDI is as a back-up to manual services in order to obtain coverage of material not taken by the unit, or to supply references on fringe topics not scanned for.

The clue to present attitudes about current awareness services and to future plans for provision can be plainly read in the literature describing practice during this period. *The early seventies proved to be a turning point, with economic factors replacing the needs of the users as the number one priority.*

## The survey findings

The survey covered a total of 33 information units, large and 'small', to 13 of which personal visits were made. The survey letter and details of how it was carried out are in Appendix 1. Appendix 2 gives a list of respondents, and indicates what visits were made.

## Computerisation and CAS

Computerisation was widespread. Twenty-nine of the 33 units surveyed were using computers — not just for current awareness service, but also to access on-line databases, for word processing, in the development and use of in-house databases, or for computer conferencing.

Information units of the larger organisations tend to exploit the company mainframe or minicomputers. Local area networks have been set up in some organisations, making information available to professionals via computer terminals at their workplace. These can be used to obtain access to the organisation's own databases, or to commercial databases. For instance Rolls-Royce operate a network of 300 terminals, using IBM STAIRS software. Unilever has networks at Colworth House and Port Sunlight, where a variety of databases can be searched with their own VIEWDECO software. At the Atomic Energy Research Establishment, Harwell, there is a network incorporating STATUS information retrieval software. Smaller units (in terms of numbers of clients and budget provision, that is) have purchased micro-computers or word processor systems. The word processors are used as a terminal for on-line communication as well as for text manipulation.

Eighteen out of 29 units are using a computer in *bulletin production*. A hard-copy bulletin is produced in all cases, but four units make their bulletin available on-line as well. References are input to the computer in random order, as the literature is scanned. Bulletin output is obtained at the appropriate time by sorting and printing, with the addition of subject headings or cross references if required. For instance, at British Steel a WORDPLEX 80/85 system with disc storage, and capable of supporting four terminals, is used to input 300-400 references per month. These are sorted to produce 18 SDI bulletins, each with up to five sections – all in a half to one hour! It is not just a question of speed, however, because using the word processor means that more breakdown of the references is possible with sections and headings. The Electricity Council uses a micro to input and edit the bulletin. Then the text is transferred to an ICL mainframe which produces the bulletin masters. At the Fire Research Station a monthly bulletin is produced for internal use, but the references are retained and collated into a quarterly abstracts journal, which is sold outside. At Allied Breweries it was found that by using their micro for bulletin production, the same number of staff could cope with the workload, even though the amount of material to be processed had increased. Furthermore, they are able to produce a bulletin fortnightly now, instead of monthly as before, and they have the time to include longer abstracts.

Material selected for a bulletin is not necessarily discarded after bulletin preparation. Many information units can see the benefit of creating an in-house database with the same input that goes to produce the bulletin. This is then used for retrospective searches. In some places a database built from scanning the current literature is a commercial activity. For instance at Harwell the scanning done in the information section contributes towards the databases associated with five specialised information centres. At the GLC Research Library a database of news items on urban matters is used for an internal bulletin, but also made available outside.

A few organisations have made their information bulletin available on-line. At UKAEA, Harwell, an experimental bulletin has been mounted on the local network, and is available directly to a number of professionals around the site. However, widespread use of an on-line bulletin is seen as taking five to ten years, as professionals of the 'punched card' generation retire and younger people with a background of on-line computing come into the organisation. The GLC news bulletin is available on-line within the organisation, but also to the public via a database host.

Generally speaking, the on-line bulletin is seen as being more flexible than a paper bulletin. It can be read when the customer pleases. It gives the opportunity of presenting information on a topic rather than current information – the distinction between current awareness and retrospective search is blurred. It gives the user the possibility of choice by section or by topic, rather than always having to scan an entire issue. Ultimately an on-line bulletin will enable wider dissemination than a paper bulletin with its distribution list. However to use an on-line bulletin one does need access to a terminal, and one has to make the effort to sit in front of it and log on to the system. In contrast the paper bulletin can be read any time, any place, anywhere.

What is perhaps more important, it appears on your desk, demanding to be looked at. The ability to search for just those items the client feels will be relevant to his or her interests is a two-edged sword. In browsing through a paper bulletin one comes across items under different headings which are relevant to one's work. Also browsing is useful because other material, not necessarily sought but nevertheless stimulating to one's ideas is found. It was obvious from the survey that those who supply their bulletin on-line were thinking about the negative aspects of on-line bulletin presentation, and no doubt answers to these major drawbacks will be found. Should the on-line bulletin be allowed to substitute entirely for a visit to the library to browse through current material? This question was posed by one respondent.

The provision of *personal notifications* from in-house scanning was curiously not a feature of the mechanised services surveyed, except in one case, where material input for a bulletin was also searched for personal interests. However, at GEC-Marconi Electronics a database of information service users and their interests is planned, searchable by subject. This will provide a useful referral device, to find experts on any subject.

Specialised databases in the organisations surveyed were not restricted to references from current literature. Many units maintain indexed databases to internal reports. British Steel have plans to develop a database on what their competitors are doing. Unilever (Colworth House) have a database on an aspect of food legislation. These databases are also a source of current awareness for employees, since they are kept up to date with new information.

To summarise, the survey has shown that computerisation of current awareness services in large and small information units has expanded, and is continuing to expand, with an ever-increasing reliance on the ability of mechanisation to integrate information unit activities with each other, and with the customers of the unit, via a local network. However the primary motive for such expansion has been economic: the desire to provide a cost-efficient information service, of which current awareness is just one aspect. If there have been advantages to current awareness itself, these are mainly in reducing the labour costs associated with bulletin production, or bulletin/index production, thus making the provision of a current awareness service *in-house* a more attractive option. Whereas in the 1970s the response of smaller information units to demands for more cost-efficient operation was to let staff go and use SDI from computerised secondary services, microcomputers seem to have enabled a more self-reliant attitude to current awareness services to be maintained.

### Use of primary and secondary sources

Present-day approaches to current awareness service are as diverse as they were in the 1970s. Among the larger organisations, rejection of primary literature scanning as the main source of references is more widespread, however. Provision of a service from numerous tapes spun at a central department has been the approach at ICI for a long time now. Four hundred to 500 profiles are run per week and distributed to the divisional laboratories. Some divisions of ICI are aware of the limitations of this arrangement, but will live with its deficiencies because it is alleged to be 'cost-effective'. The information staff at individual laboratories spend time on enquiry work in place of scanning primary literature. On the other hand, search profiles for the machine SDI are updated only on demand. At British Gas part of the current awareness service is from a shared database supported by local scanning at the divisions, so the position is not so extreme as at ICI (although, of course, the subject distribution is different).

In contrast to the labour-intensive process of manually scanning the primary literature, computerised secondary services offer information units an easy and cost-efficient method of keeping its customers currently informed. What is conveniently ignored is the lack of effectiveness of SDI from commercial databases, and the extent to which the users receive any benefit from this approach to current awareness. The respondent from British Gas summed up the situation facing many of the larger organisations in the provision of a current awareness service: 'current awareness, although desirable, is very labour intensive, and in a situation of reduced staffing it has to compete in the priority stakes with all the other services expected of an industrial/technical information unit'.

Two of the larger company information services have more recently moved away from primary literature scanning. For example, at Unilever Research (Port Sunlight) the SDI bulletins and personal notifications which have been supplied since the early 1960s were disbanded in 1981. Current awareness of internal reports is still intact but as regards current literature there are the few on-line profiles which were run before the bulletin was abandoned plus some batch SDI from UKCIS and some CA Selects. At Shell Central Library a bulletin from scanning the primary literature was replaced recently by bulletins bought in from outside. The needs of individuals are met by on-line profiles which they operate themselves. The attitude of senior management in both cases is that the professional workers will keep themselves informed on current events in those areas important to them. However it is acknowledged (by the professionals themselves) that in many cases this will not happen.

Twenty-eight of the 33 information units in the survey maintain scanning of primary literature sources as input to their current awareness services. The importance of primary sources is explained by the comments received from individual units. For example, at the Marine Biological Association (Plymouth) current awareness service from primary sources is given priority because an immediate, very personal service is possible — something that commercial services could never supply. Also the MBA service has a relatively small number of clients (60), and it can rely on its own intake of the subject literature. The Mining Research and Development Establishment (Burton-on-Trent) library also has a relatively small number of clients. Here a bulletin and in-house mechanised SDI is produced, both from primary literature scanning. Scanning is not confined to the 'smaller' units, however. For example, Rolls-Royce maintain manual scanning, supplemented by regular on-line searches. At British Steel one information unit serves three divisions, and 18 SDI bulletins are produced from primary literature input.

It seems that the desire for cost-efficiency has been balanced by a concern that an effective and beneficial service is produced. The information service must do for the clients what the clients might never do for themselves. Comments from several units point to deficiencies in secondary services which prevent their wholesale adoption for current awareness: the delay in compilation of secondary services, the difficulty of writing computer search profiles to cover wide or vaguely defined interests, the fact that browsing on-line is extremely expensive, if not actually impossible. Two units mentioned an additional factor which predisposes them towards primary literature use. On-line use of secondary services represents an extra, very visible, cost — no matter whether it is done by the information service or the clients!

Twelve out of the 33 units surveyed use a combination of primary and secondary sources for current awareness. At Esso Research (Abingdon) bulletins from primary sources provide a rapid alerting service on material actually purchased. As regards wider coverage it is considered that on-line SDI is better for the scientist, who might not be able to select material so easily from printed secondary sources. However the search profile has to be correct, and there are drawbacks associated with frequent changes in client's interests and the large number of items that need to be obtained from outside if profiles are run frequently.

Fisons and Bush Boake Allen both use secondary sources to supplement their scanning of the literature for bulletin production. For example, material from the Derwent patents abstracts is extracted for inclusion in a bulletin. Some computerised SDI is taken from commercial databases, on topics not scanned for the bulletins. It also serves as a back-up in those areas where complete coverage is essential.

Roussel Laboratories were not running SDI profiles on-line. In this decision they were influenced by the research done by Blick at Beechams, where he compared computerised SDI and journal scanning as sources of material for current awareness services (Blick 1972). Hence Roussel scan current journals, patents abstracts, *Current Contents, Current Abstracts of Chemistry/Index Chemicus* and other printed sources. Although time-consuming, journal scanning allows

82

vaguely related material to be recognised. Slight changes in direction of research interests can be easily accommodated. These are things that a computer cannot equal. In contrast, Wellcome Research Laboratories have around 200 profiles running on a variety of computer-based services, as well as internal scanning.

The in-house scanning of journals and secondary publications at UKAEA Harwell feeds the needs of· a variety of individuals and projects. A weekly information bulletin is produced in hard copy and electronic form. The scanning also provides references for five specialist information centres on site, and for Harwell's input to the International Nuclear Information System database. In return the unit is able to use output tapes from INIS twice a month to run profiles for SDI. While Harwell uses a combination of primary and secondary sources, they feel that if you provide current awareness it is important that the information *is* current, and not three to six months old.

Unilever Research (Colworth House) offers a contrast to the research laboratory at Port Sunlight in that at present the input of references to their bulletins is about 90 per cent from scanning of primary literature. About 140 profiles are run in-house from ISI tapes, this service being taken up more by the basic research groups. The bulletins are available on the campus network as well as in hard copy. However, directions have come from senior management to rely more on secondary services, and yet to penetrate more deeply into research programmes, and be seen to be contributing to their success. This is indeed a challenge, which the unit at Colworth House is in the process of picking up.

In summary, the use of secondary sources for current awareness service is on the increase, but different units see their use in different ways. For example, they allow Shell and ICI to dispense with a great deal of manual scanning, Fisons to extend literature coverage beyond that achievable with manual scanning, and Harwell to serve a different type of client need. However, scanning of the primary literature still dominates the current awareness scene, with production of an information bulletin or SDI bulletins or even, in units with a high scanner to client ratio, personal notifications. The decision to retain manual scanning does not appear to be related to size of information service. Certainly, part of the reason for scanning the primary literature, despite the cost, is a desire to give effective service.

### The influence of management

The age of 'new technology' alone is not sufficient to explain the large-scale movement towards computerisation, and the associated move towards the use of secondary services for current awareness. Part of the praise, or blame, has to be laid at the door of senior management, whose needs to introduce more cost-efficiency into company operations have to be acted upon by middle managers such as librarians and information officers.

In its most extreme form the need of senior management for cost-efficiency has caused the complete abandonment of information services. This has been going on since the early 1970s. A recent fatality was the information service at United Glass Containers, which was discontinued 'as part of a series of measures designed to overcome severe economic and financial problems'. This sort of thing could happen to almost any service, however useful, because each time it needs to make economies senior management looks at departments without obvious cash outputs — the typing pool, the personnel department, the canteen. Now it is the turn of 'the library'.

A less extreme approach is for management to 'interfere' in the operation or organisation of an existing information service, by looking askance at manual operations, and pointing to the increased cost-efficiency of computerisation. For example, senior management at Shell and Unilever (Port Sunlight) have forced information units to disband in-house provision of current awareness because they saw the manual scanning involved as labour-intensive and noticeably costly. At Shell a move towards heavy reliance on secondary services was fully justified in the eyes of management because they felt that the customers of the present service had no need for current information. The current awareness service was a back-up to ensure that nothing of importance had been missed. If up-to-the-minute information is required, the customers can obtain that far more easily themselves from the FT index or Reuters on-line. At Unilever (Port Sunlight) the abandonment of in-house current awareness was justified on the grounds that it would be more beneficial if scientists did their own scanning of the literature. The fact that the management conference that made the decision was concerned with cost savings clearly illustrates the true motivation behind their action.

At ICI (Petrochemicals and Plastics Division) pressure is exerted from above not to increase staff numbers, and to buy in outside services wherever possible. At Unilever (Colworth House) management appears to be attempting to redefine the whole concept of the information unit. It is now part of the computer services department. Although the visit there was made part way through a time of change, it seemed to be set on course to become more of an enabling unit than an information service.

Nevertheless, it appears from the survey that not all management is hell-bent on forcing cost-efficiency at any price in benefit and effectiveness. Many of the respondents had not been pressed for economies of this sort, and had nothing to report about higher management intervention. The pharmaceutical companies among the survey respondents had fared well. For instance, at Beechams the head of information services had sought to demonstrate the superiority of a current awareness service based on in-house scanning compared with use of online databases for current awareness, and management had accepted his findings. At Fisons and Smith Kline & French, money is available for development of in-house databases as well as for current awareness services.

Generally speaking, where action has been taken by senior management in the name of cost-efficiency, it has had a deleterious effect on current awareness service. The information units in organisations where senior management is content to take a more passive role, or where the benefits of complete information are seen as vital to company survival, are the ones which have profited from the 1980s. They have had money made available for computers and yet have been able to retain traditional, more effective current awareness methods as well.

## Conclusions

Looking first at the present, the greatest contrast with the past is the establishment of computers in information units of all sizes. This phenomenon is directly related to higher management's concern with cost-efficiency within an organisation. It could be said to be the advantageous aspect of this concern.

For the majority of information units surveyed, who scan the current primary literature and produce a bulletin, computers mean that time can be saved in bulletin compilation, and that the production of current awareness notifications can be made more flexible. New technology also means the possibility of a local network, on which current information can be used as soon as it has been extracted from the literature. More immediate access is possible to new information, and also wider dissemination of the material occurs. The professional of the future will be able to find and read the current awareness file as part of a daily routine − that of accessing a computer. Computerisation also makes it easy to build up an in-house database of material extracted for current awareness, in addition to files of internal information. This in turn improves access to the sort of information that is perennially useful to an organisation, since it can be indexed and searched in a manner most appropriate to the need.

However, higher management's concern with cost-efficiency can be seen, particularly in some of the larger organisations, to have a disadvantageous aspect as well. This happens in cases where scanning of primary literature is discouraged or forbidden, or where the word is passed down that professionals must in future keep up to date by their own efforts. This interference has the effect in the first case of reducing the effectiveness of a current awareness service by removing input from primary sources, and in the second case of removing all the benefit to the professional of having his literature scanning done for him as well as the benefit of those useful inputs to his or her work that result.

(Whitehall's work on the Harwell and Trent Polytechnic bulletins shows that the sum of benefits from these inputs can in fact greatly exceed the cost of bulletin production, but that in its absence most clients would be unable to do enough scanning to replace the bulletin service. Some quite senior people were found to benefit from the bulletin, but would be unable to spend any time on current awareness if it was discontinued.)

The temptation to try to predict the future is irresistible, despite the lessons of the past. Worth quoting is Cronin's opinion that developments within larger corporations represent the leading edge of IT applications, and that it does not necessarily follow that an equal level of sophistication will become the norm. Perhaps the larger companies will find some way of making their enforced reliance on secondary sources more effective, or try to temper their client's enforced self-sufficiency with measures which encourage them to keep up to date, and increase the likelihood of their obtaining benefit. As for the rest of us, there seems no good reason at the moment why the current awareness bulletin and personal notifications, compiled from a mixture of primary and secondary sources, should not continue.

A hope for the future would be that senior management within industry should heed the example set by their information managers, and have more concern for the cost and benefit of operations as opposed to their present concern for cost-efficiency. The importance of current information to industry really is too great to be sacrificed to cost-efficiency alone.

### References

Anthony, L. J. et al. 'Selective dissemination of information using a KDF9 computer', *Aslib Proceedings*, January 1968, 40–64.

Arnold, D. V. 'Structure of information services', *Aslib Proceedings*, December 1972, 654–63.

Blick, A. R., Magrill, D. S., 'The value of a weekly in-house current awareness bulletin serving pharmaceutical research scientists', *Information Scientist*, March 1975, 19–28.

Blick, A. R. et al., 'A comparison of online databases with a large in-house information bulletin in the provision of current awareness', *Journal of Information Science*, May 1982, 79–86.

Cronin, B. 'Adaption, extinction or genetic drift', *Aslib Proceedings*, June/July 1983, 278–89.

Dammers, H. F., 'Industrial information services', in *Chemical Information Systems*, ed. Ash J., Hyde, E., Ellis Horwood, 1975, 13–31.

East, H., 'The development of SDI services', *Aslib Proceedings*, November 1968, 482–91.

Haygarth-Jackson, A. R., 'Utilisation of mechanised services', *Information Scientist*, vol. 6, 1972, 132–8.

Luhn, H. P., 'A business intelligence system', *IBM Journal of Research and Development*, October 1958, 314–19.

Luhn, H. P., 'Selective dissemination of new scientific information with the aid of electronic processing equipment', *American Documentation*, April 1961, 131–8.

Nightingale, R. A., 'A cost-benefit study of a manually-produced current awareness service', *Aslib Proceedings*, April 1973, 153–7.

Rogers, J. A., 'An examination of the development of current awareness services within industrial information units', Master's Dissertation, Loughborough University of Technology, 1985.

Saunderson, M., 'The information function in relation to user departments: an excursion into the future', *Aslib Proceedings*, February 1977, 77–90.

Terry, T. E., Jones, P. J., 'The use of external databases to extend current awareness services based on internal resources at AERE, Harwell', *Aslib Proceedings*, December 1972, 672–7.

Whitehall, T., 'Cost, value and effectiveness of current awareness service', in *Practical Current Awareness Services from Libraries*, ed. Whitehall, T., Gower 1986.

## Appendix 1
### Method used for the survey

A letter (reproduced below) was sent to 70 information units in the UK. Forty replies were received, 33 of them containing useful information. Twenty respondents offered the chance of a visit to their unit. In the time available thirteen visits were made, and these are listed in Appendix II. The interviews on each visit followed the same pattern as the questions in the letter.

---

Dept. of Library and Information Studies
The Pilkington Library
Loughborough University of Technology
Loughborough
Leics. LE11 3HT

4th June 1985

Dear Sir/Madam,

I am a postgraduate student at Loughborough University of Technology following an M.A. in Library and Information Studies. I would be grateful if you could help me with my thesis on how current awareness services have developed over the last 7-10 years.

Since Tom Whitehall's survey on current awareness for the British Library in 1976, there have been many developments in libraries, with micro computers coming to the fore and databases being integrated into the special library service. My thesis is chiefly concerned with the following questions. (a) How the greater availability of computers has affected the current awareness service. (b) The effect of the wider availability of secondary services through commercial databases, on current awareness service. (c) Lastly, I wanted to give serious consideration to the problems and opportunities that management has encountered because of such technological developments within the field of information: by this I mean management of library information services as well as senior management.

From my pilot interviews I can see that I should be collecting informed comment on the following topics. Are any of these relevant to your own situation?

As regards computers, I am interested in how long they have been part of the current awareness service and for what purpose they have been employed. Can the use of computers improve current awareness or save money? Is anything lost by employing a computer compared to the more traditional methods of current awareness? What future developments do you envisage for the use of computers as part of a current awareness service?

88

For current awareness do you place the emphasis on primary or secondary sources, manual or online scanning procedures, and why? Do you use on-line commercial databases, and how are they used? What combination (primary, secondary, manual, online) achieves the best results — 'best' for the management of scarce resources, and 'best' for the clients' needs. I am interested in what type of service you provide (bulletins, personal notification) and how you produce it. What is the trade off between cost and effectiveness of different approaches?

The managerial problems that may have been created with the advent of new technology and methods within the special library. The cost of accessing commercial databases, or the buying of computers — again the trade off between cost and effectiveness. How can one tell whether the service is achieving what it purports to be doing?

I would be most grateful if you could spend a little time in writing to me about your current awareness service. If current awareness is inappropriate in your situation, I would be interested in the rationale of this.

I am also looking for opportunities to discuss these questions with a practising librarian/Information Officer and would be grateful for an hour or two of your time it you think it would be useful.

Please accept my appreciation for any help which you can give. I hope to start writing at the beginning of July 1985.

Yours sincerely

Jane A. Rogers

### Appendix 2
### Respondents to the survey

Allied Breweries, Burton-on-Trent
Beecham Pharmaceuticals Research Division, Brockham Park, Betch-
    worth, Surrey
British Gas Research & Development Division, Midlands
British Gas Research & Development Division, North East
*British Steel Corporation, Swindon Laboratories, Rotherham
*Bush Boake Allen Ltd, London
Colgate Palmolive, Salford
Davy McKee, Sheffield
*Electricity Council, London
Esso Refinery, Fawley
Esso Research Centre, Abingdon
Fire Research Association, Borehamwood, Herts.
*Fisons Pharmaceuticals, Loughborough

GEC, Marconi Research Centre, Essex
Gillette Industries, Reading
*GLC Research Library, London
ICI Mond Division, Cheshire
ICI Organics Division, Manchester
*ICI Petrochemicals and Plastics Division, Middlesborough
IMI, Wilton, Birmingham
*Marine Biological Association, Plymouth
*Mining Research & Development Establishment, Burton
Ministry of Agriculture & Fisheries, Slough
Rolls-Royce, Derby
Roussel Laboratories (UK) Ltd., Swindon
*Shell Centre, Central Information & Library, London
Smith Kline & French, Welwyn Garden City
*Thorne EMI Central Research Laboratories, Hayes, Middlesex
United Glass, St Albans
*United Kingdom Atomic Energy Authority, Harwell
*Unilever Research, Colworth House, Sharnbrook, Beds.
*Unilever Research, Port Sunlight, Wirral
Wellcome Research Laboratories, Langley Court, Beckenham, Kent.


* A visit was made to the organisations marked with an asterisk.

# 7      Cost, value and effectiveness of current awareness service

## Tom Whitehall

This is an account of evaluations of information bulletins produced at Trent Polytechnic and UKAEA, Harwell — with a focus on the methods used for evaluation rather than on the bulletins themselves.

Attempts to evaluate a service of any sort may be made for a number of reasons, but the most usual is the desire to show that the time and money that go into producing the service are not wasted — that there is as a result some useful impact on the people who make use of it. This was the situation at Trent Polytechnic, where the chief executive had questioned the value of a weekly news bulletin covering further, higher and adult education. (The efficiency of production of the bulletin was not in question. The point at issue was whether the benefit obtained by its readers was worth the resources consumed in producing it.) At Harwell it was costing a great deal to print 500 copies of a technical bulletin, and the information officer was concerned about the benefit being obtained from such a costly operation.

Another common reason for evaluation is for the provider of a service to know that it satisfies the needs of its users for effect and for convenience in use. (Quality control of a product for the industrial or retail market is perhaps a good analogy.) Such a situation had arisen at Trent because this bulletin was about to become a co-operative effort with two other organisations, each of whom produced a bulletin on similar topics. The need was to investigate the effectiveness of the bulletin at a time when a change in bulletin compilation was envisaged. At Harwell a survey of photocopies requested had shown that interest in the more 'serious' journal articles reported in the bulletin was low.

### Techniques for determining value

Fortunately we have a clear indication of how cost must be calculated for use in a cost-benefit comparison. The relevant costs are 'the costs which would not be incurred if the service was not provided' (Flowerdew and Whitehead 1974). In the case of an information bulletin this means the cost of any materials bought especially for the bulletin, and of any labour undertaken in its production, or as a direct consequence of its production. So the cost of periodicals scanned for the bulletin which would be bought whether the bulletin was produced or not is not relevant. On the other hand, the costs in labour and materials of supplying copies of articles in response to bulletin users' requests *are* relevant, since if there was no bulletin these costs would not be incurred.

A number of different approaches to obtaining estimates of the value of information bulletins have been reported or suggested:

(a) *Time saved studies*: The value of a bulletin is equated with the time its users would need to spend in keeping up with the current literature if the bulletin was not provided. Nightingale (1973) and Blick and Magrill (1975) describe examples of this type of study.

A serious criticism of 'time saved' studies of information bulletins is that the studies reported so far appear to assume that all recipients of a bulletin actually make some use of it, so that each recipient is credited with some time saved. This is a bold assumption to make. Assumptions are also made about the number of journals clients would scan in the absence of the bulletin, or about the time they would spend in doing their own current awareness scanning. These assumptions have caused some writers to be very critical of what seems a promising technique for indicating value. In the studies made at Trent and at Harwell the method was modified to receive more client input. Each client was asked what s/he would do in the absence of the bulletin. If they admitted to doing some scanning to replace it, clients were asked how much they would do, and the cost of the time this would take was calculated as the alternative cost.

(b) *Cost from another source*: The cost of a similar publication, but from a commercial source (or the recipients' idea of what this cost would be) has been used to represent the value of an information bulletin. Martyn's (1980) study uses this measure of value.

These approaches both use the idea of 'alternative cost': In the absence of the service what would it cost the client to avail himself of the next best alternative?

(c) *'Prepared to pay' studies*: The bulletin recipient is asked what s/he would pay to retain the service, and this amount is taken as its value to the recipient: for instance Morley and Hopkins' (1969) study of an information bulletin for social scientists at the University of Durham. Here the problem was that the amounts offered by respondents were very small in comparison with the production cost of the bulletin.

(d) *Time spent on the service*: Orr (1970) has suggested that the amount of time a recipient is prepared to spend in making use of a service can be used as an indication of its value to him. This seems to be a reasonable view, since professional workers would be expected to think twice before wasting their working time. The time 'spent' on making use of a current awareness service could be spent elsewhere — on project work, for instance.

(e) *Value of information received*: In a quite different approach to justification of information bulletins, an attempt is made to find a cash value not for the bulletin itself, but for the facts or ideas that recipients of the bulletin service have obtained by making use of it. For instance Martyn (1980) tried to obtain a value for the bulletin supplied by Leicester City Libraries to executives at County Hall by asking the recipients to give the annual cash value of its contribution to their work. The values he obtained were very small (£20 per annum or so) and suggest that the respondents had not thought about how information gained via the bulletin had interacted with their work. In the value for money studies at Trent and Harwell it was decided to ask the bulletin recipients first to describe ways in which they had used information obtained via the bulletin, and then to attempt to ascribe a value to it in terms of work time saved or advantage gained.

To estimate the value of a current awareness service, we need to add the value of information received and put to use which is apparent from use of method (e) to the value of the service itself found by using one of the methods (a) to (d).


### Techniques for determining effectiveness

The determination of the effectiveness of library and information services is in its infancy, partly because 'effectiveness' has been confused with 'efficiency' and thought of in terms of intermediate output (numbers of services given or made available) and not in terms of the satisfaction of quality criteria which apply to individual services. However the literature of *evaluation* of services does supply quality criteria, based on the aspects of a service which are most closely related to client satisfaction (Whitehall 1984). For current awareness service these are as follows:

Coverage of the topics of interest to the client, by means of scanning the appropriate range and type of literature.

Timeliness, in terms of the delay time between first publication of an item and its notification to the clients.

Relevance of the items presented to the client by the service.

Content of notifications (which clients use in a judgement of whether it is worth their while arranging to see a copy of the original).

Back-up (the ease with which a client is able to refer to a copy of the item notified).

The evaluations at Trent and Harwell established that for bulletins, as opposed to personal notifications, there are two other criteria connected with client satisfaction:

Bulletin format and arrangement, which make the bulletin easy to scan.

Reading load, or bulletin size and frequency.

There are no generally-accepted standards for these criteria, against which the bulletins could be measured — such standards would not be appropriate for all the criteria. The technique adopted was first of all to ask the known readers of the bulletin what aspects they regarded as good or bad about the bulletin service. Then, when they had talked about the features that were uppermost in their minds, a checklist of aspects which covered all the above criteria was used to obtain their comments on each. In this way any shortcomings of the bulletins would become apparent.

### How the evaluations at Trent and Harwell were made

(a) *Finding the cost of the bulletins*

At Trent one librarian scanned current material and also keyboarded items into the computer at convenient times during the week. A printout was obtained each fortnight, with the items rearranged in alphabetical order of subject heading. An assistant copied the pages of printout, attached a cover-sheet, and distributed the issues. The other cost associated with the bulletin was the cost of photocopies made in response to requests from bulletin readers.

Labour costs were obtained for these operations by recording in diary form the time spent on the activities involved in bulletin production over several months, then calculating the proportion of his working time each person spent, and multiplying by the annual salary. (Since costs and benefits were to be compared within the same establishment, no overheads were included in the salary figures.) Materials costs were for copy paper, the bulletin cover sheets, and one copy of the HERTIS bulletin, which was used as a secondary source of items for the Trent bulletin. Details of the costing are shown in Table 1. In calculating labour costs, the proportion of total working time spent on an activity was obtained by using a denominator of 100,000 minutes, equivalent to seven and a quarter hours per day for 230 days per year.

Finding the scanning cost at Harwell was more difficult, because the weekly information bulletin is only one of the outputs from the information office. It was estimated that one-seventh of the total cost of scanning contributed to the bulletin. This is because if the bulletin was not produced most of the scanning effort would continue since it contributes to the INIS database and an extensive SDI service as well as providing input to the specialised information centres at Harwell. Other costs were keyboarding and checking the bulletin masters.

The cost per copy at Trent was £1.25, or £31 per annum. At Harwell the cost was £1.60 per copy or £80 per annum.

(b) *Finding the value of the bulletins, and their effectiveness*

There are good reasons why people attempting to evaluate a service should be prepared to talk to the users of the service, rather than send them a questionnaire. Interviewees can be encouraged to

## Table 1

### Details of costing for *Education News*

The activities involved are scanning, keyboarding the references, and copying, collation and distribution. The cost of the photocopy service which results from the bulletin is included, as an avoidable cost.

1. *SCANNING*

   Labour cost: 1,375 mins. per annum
   $$@ £7,650 = 1,375/100,000 \times 7,650$$
   $$= £105$$
   Materials cost: One copy of HERTIS
   $$= £10.50$$

   *Total scanning cost*      £115.50

2. *KEYBOARDING*

   Labour cost: 10,479 mins per annum
   $$@ £7,650 = 10,479/100,000 \times 7,650$$
   $$= £802$$

   *Total keyboarding cost*      £802.00

3. *COPYING/COLLATION/DISTRIBUTION*

   Labour cost: 7,909 mins per annum
   $$@ £4,960 = 7,909/100,000 \times 4,960$$
   $$= £392$$
   Materials cost: 1,250 covers per annum @ £27.20 per 2,000
   $$= 1,250/2,000 \times 27.20$$
   $$= £17$$
   1,820 sheets copy paper per annum @ £1.50 per 500
   $$= 1,820/500 \times 1.5$$
   $$= £5$$

   *Total processing cost*      £414.00

4. *PHOTOCOPYING IN RESPONSE TO BULLETIN*

   Labour cost: 4,500 mins per annum
   $$@ £4,960 = 4,500/100,000 \times 4,960$$
   $$= £223$$
   Materials cost: 1,500 sheets copy paper per annum
   $$= 1,500/500 \times 1.5$$
   $$= £4.50$$

   *Total photocopying cost*      £227.50

   *Total cost of bulletin service, per annum*      £1,559.00

answer the questions intended, yet other observations, not called for by the questionnaire but nevertheless of value, can be received and understood. Any enthusiasm a respondent may have for the service comes across more clearly in an interview (as does irony and prevarication). One sees the user in his natural surroundings, and gains from this. Hunches and insights can be confirmed or denied more easily by observing the user face to face. Probably the greatest challenge of the interview situation is to get what you want and at the same time attempt to prevent your respondent from giving you the cosy answer s/he imagines you expect. Its greatest value, in my opinion, lies in the explanations that the respondent can give you, and in what you are told by the form of words s/he uses.

To obtain an estimate of value, one needs ideally to talk to each recipient of the bulletin who puts it to use — that is to say, reads it regularly. Each user will have some estimate of its value, and the challenge is to discover what this is. We cannot assume that all users value the bulletin to the same extent. Certainly we cannot assume that the bulletin is valued by all who *receive* it.

An effectiveness survey also needs to be carried out among users rather than recipients of the service. This is because people who do not make use of a service are unlikely to be able to tell you about its shortcomings from a user's point of view! On the other hand, one does not have to attempt to talk to *all* users, since after only a few interviews any serious problems with the bulletin will have been revealed. An exception to this general rule would be if it were considered necessary to gather a range of opinion on a particular aspect of the bulletin.

At Trent only about 50 people received a copy of the bulletin, so it was possible to start with the aim of talking to all the recipients, and using information from the subset who were discovered to be users. At Harwell there were about 500 recipients, so a sample had to be taken.

The librarian at Trent wrote to bulletin recipients, asking them to accept an interview in the interests of checking the effectiveness of the bulletin. Regular users, identified by their requests for photocopies, were telephoned to fix an interview date. A note was put on the front cover of the bulletin over several issues asking recipients to mark items which they had found relevant to their interests, and to return the bulletin copies, which would be replaced if need be. These approaches led to 19 offers of interviews and five refusals. A short questionnaire was sent to the remaining recipients, asking whether they made any use of their copy of the bulletin, and if so what sort of use. Ten more interviews were obtained by this means, and eight non-users. Two recipients scanned the bulletin but did not offer an interview, and four did not reply to any of the overtures.

It is not easy to discover who makes use of an information bulletin. At least three extra users were found who were not on the official circulation list. On the other hand it was strongly suspected as a result of some of the interviews that a few alleged users did not, in fact, make any use of their copy of the bulletin. (One of the features of the Trent bulletin which nearly every respondent complained about was its arrangement — however some of the 'regular users' had not noticed how it was arranged! In another case it was obvious that a respondent had used the bulletin for the first time when marking the trial copies.)

At Harwell there had already been a preliminary survey of bulletin recipients, and the results of this were used to select users for the value and effectiveness interviews. One of the questions had been about the ease of use of the bulletin. Another asked the recipients to rate its value to them on a scale:

Indispensable — very valuable — not very valuable — of little value

Just over half the recipients were able to answer these questions, and it was assumed that these were the users of the bulletin. A sample of 30 users was taken which represented in proportion the ratings of bulletin value.


### Success of the 'value' questions

(a) *The alternative cost of keeping up with the literature*

Clients who admitted to reading their copy of the bulletin were asked, 'If you did not have the bulletin, how would you go about keeping up with new material on the topics it covers?' Nine bulletin users at Trent admitted that they would spend time to replace the bulletin as a source of current awareness, varying from 30 minutes to four hours per week. This time was converted to cash at the individual's salary rate. The alternative cost to nine users (of a bulletin whose production cost for 50 copies was £1,559) was found to be £6,550. At Harwell 22 of the 30 interviewees would do some scanning in the absence of the bulletin, varying from 30 minutes to five hours per week. The alternative cost to 22 of the approximately 260 users was £25,000 per annum, compared with a bulletin cost of £40,000 in all (£1,760 for the 22 copies).

Finding the alternative cost of keeping up thus appears to be a successful technique for obtaining figures for the value of a bulletin. However, in a few cases clients who read the bulletin and admitted to its usefulness in their work said that they would be unable to spend time in scanning to replace it, because they would be unable to afford any time. These were all quite senior people, and it is a pity that this method does not record an alternative cost to them. The connection between alternative cost of a client's scanning and value of the bulletin to him is confirmed by those cases in which clients would do no work to replace it because they regarded the bulletin as an extra — 'It's like the nine o'clock news', 'It's a bonus'. About half the users at Trent were librarians, who came into this category because they already did some scanning and used the bulletin as a backstop.

From the point of view of calculating alternative cost it is better to have from clients the *time* they would spend on scanning, rather than the number of publications they would scan. On the other hand if they can name the material they would have to seek out and go through, it provides a more convincing demonstration of value.

### (b) *The cost of an alternative from a commercial source*

The cost per person per annum of the bulletin at Trent was £31 and at Harwell £80. Users were asked to say what they imagined a bulletin like this would cost from a commercial source. The replies at both Trent and Harwell had a wide spread, due to some very high valuations from one or two respondents. I would guess that clients were using a range of different valuation criteria. If the very high valuations were ignored and a mean value was taken it was found that Trent users value their bulletin at £10 per annum in excess of its cost, and Harwell users at just below its cost. Respondents found this a difficult question to answer, and there were many refusals.

### (c) *What users were prepared to pay for the bulletin*

Users were asked what was the most they would pay for their regular copy of the bulletin if they had to pay for it with money from their departmental funds, thus having less to spend on other provisions. At Trent 23 clients would pay a total of £665 per annum for the bulletin (the cost for 23 clients was £713 per annum). At Harwell nine clients would pay a total of £1,950 per annum. (Cost for nine clients was £720.) At Trent, where most of the known users answered the question, it can be seen that the method gives a valuation which approximates to the bulletin cost.

### (d) *Respondents' time spent in making use of the service*

Recipients who admitted to scanning the bulletin were asked to record how long this took. For each client the mean of three measurements was taken, and converted to cash at the salary rate. A few respondents used the bulletin in some other way — indexing it or cutting and pasting items from it, and so an estimate of how long they spent on these operations was obtained. Many clients obtained photocopies of bulletin items as a result of scanning the bulletin and read them. Some clients indexed these copies as well. Times spent on these bulletin-related activities were obtained, and converted to cash at the salary rate.

At Trent 30 clients spent a total of £1,597 of their working time on the bulletin service. (Cost of the bulletin for 30 people was £930.)

At Harwell 23 clients spent £3,068 of their time. (Cost of the bulletin for 23 clients was £1,840.)

Bearing in mind that the bulletin users could have spent their time on project work, but chose to 'spend' it on the bulletin, we can say that at both organisations the users interviewed valued the bulletin at above its cost.


(e) *Value of the bulletin as a source of information*

Bulletin users were asked to recall any items which they had seen in the bulletin, read, and which had been useful to them in connection with their work. They were asked to describe exactly how the information obtained through the bulletin item had been put to use. Ten users of the Trent bulletin and 11 users at Harwell were able to recall such items and explain how they had been useful. This technique seems to be a valuable one for justification purposes because it demonstrates many ways in which users benefit from contact with current literature. It was my feeling that the information obtained by encouraging users to think of examples was well worth the effort. Some of the responses are listed below.

> Gave evidence which was used in discussions inside and outside the polytechnic.
> Adds to the advice I can give to students.
> Provided a model for the analysis of academics' time which helped me.
> Enabled me to see how the wind is blowing.
> Helped me with the questions people fire at me.
> Enabled me to understand the different points of view on an issue.
> Provided the latest information on a changing topic.
> The information had some effect on my attitude.
> Information which was useful when we revised the course.
> An article completely changed the direction of the work we were doing. (I would never have seen it without the bulletin.)
> Information that was authoritative, and also explained things well.
> An article on the student's perception of the role of a supervisor was most useful to me.
> A starting point for my paper at a conference.
> When starting work on a new (named) topic, an article on what other people were doing gave me a quicker understanding of what were the problems.
> There was a two month delay on the delivery of some equipment. An article showed us how we could use existing equipment to do the job.
> Information about our competitors and the market for a product.

I read an article about (details given). Shortly afterwards a telephoned enquiry described a problem the answer to which I had just read.

Users who reported useful information obtained through the bulletin were asked to put a cash value on the contribution it made to their work. At Harwell five users were able to estimate project working time that had been saved. In three cases a ready-made solution to a problem was seen in print, and project time was saved equivalent to the time it would have taken to work out a solution — a computational method and program that was going to take two man-years to develop, a week or two spent trying out alternative ways of improving a corrosion test, a day or so obtaining an explanation of some absorption data. In the other two cases articles read formed the basis of new work. For instance, the time of five senior people meeting three or four times to work out what to do about a problem, writing a program on the basis of what what was read, thus saving three months work. The total cash value of the useful inputs for the five clients was £40,500 (Whitehall 1984). This is more than the annual cost of the bulletin service at Harwell.

The users at Trent found it much more difficult to give a cash value for the advantages they had obtained through items found in the bulletin, but the two responses given to the question demonstrated other approaches to quantifying value to the ones seen from the replies at Harwell. At Trent one department head credited the success so far in negotiating a £25,000 per annum project to material found via the bulletin, and said that that if his department was successful in obtaining it, this sum could be added to the value of the bulletin. Another person pointed out that her course guidelines required students to have the very latest information made available to them. This information came via the information bulletin, and in its absence the resulting disbenefit might amount to there being no course and perhaps even the loss of a member of staff.

Martyn's (1980) technique for value was tried out as a comparison. Bulletin users were asked to say what was the annual cash value of the contribution that the bulletin made to their work. On the whole this question did not, as was intended, make respondents think about the value of useful information obtained. Instead, most clients offered the alternative cost to them — the cost of the time it would take to make up for the absence of the bulletin by their own efforts. At Harwell only 11 clients answered the question; seven of these gave the alternative cost. Comments made in answer to the question were 'not so much work saved as an effect on the quality of work', 'not all the value obtained is directly related to my work', and 'It leads to ways of doing your job better'. At Trent most clients felt unable to answer the question. Five offered the alternative cost to them of the time it would take them to make up for the absence of the bulletin.

## Success of the 'effectiveness' questions

People who appeared to be making use of the bulletin were asked about its good and bad features from their own point of view, then the interviewer went through a checklist of features known to be related to quality of information bulletins:

Coverage – topics and types of material included in the bulletin.
Timeliness – Age of the bulletin items when they appeared, and items already seen by the client.
Relevance – Items that should have been included but were not. Type of item selected for the bulletin.
Ease of use – Arrangement of items, format, amount of description given with an item.
Reading load – Frequency of issues, number of items per issue.

At Trent the answers to the unprompted question revealed that clients found the bulletin arrangement, in which the same item was repeated under different subject headings, difficult to use. The page format was not liked because the headings did not stand out, and the copies (from a computer printout) appeared poorly reproduced. At Harwell the users had a different problem. The facility for ordering a copy of an item appeared not to have been worked out with bulletin users in mind. Asking for a copy to be sent involved users in a lot of writing which they were loth to undertake when a simpler method was clearly available. It was by no means necessary to interview *all* the bulletin users to discover these shortcomings. The message was clear after the first handful of interviews.

Problems that emerged in the effectiveness surveys are summarised below. (It has to be remembered that the literature habits and expectations of the readers at Trent and Harwell are quite different.)

*Coverage*. What topics, exactly, are being covered by the scanners? (Several clients wanted extra topics covered but were unsure as to the present policy for coverage.) At Harwell an interesting use situation obtains. Some clients see the bulletin as useful in supplying references on their specialist topic, whereas others see it as a service useful in covering topics *outside* their specialist area.

*Types of material scanned*. A wider range of material was called for by respondents to both the surveys. This included newspapers, books, conference reports, press releases and policy statements as well as periodical articles.

*Relevance of items*. At Trent it emerged that about a third of the respondents were less interested in items from the press than in more serious, reasoned, journal-type articles. At Harwell people mentioned the sort of item that drew one's attention to something without actually giving any useful information on it. There were comments on the importance of scanners' keeping up with people's interests.

*Ease of use*. There is a strong tendency for readers of information bulletins to look through an issue from beginning to end. Seventy per cent of the respondents at Trent did this. Here the need was for a once-only list of items, with a clear indication of where one item left off and the next one began. At Harwell a longer bulletin is arranged by journal title, with subject codes appended in the margin opposite each item. Clients scanned the issues in a variety of ways, but most looked first for journal titles. They were pleased about the new bulletin layout, with journal titles in bold type.

Most of the users at Trent wanted more description with each item: 'Sometimes I am not sure whether I have seen a bulletin item before during my own scanning' 'Cryptic titles inhibit action' 'Does the article make a statement, and if so what angle does it take?' 'Does it mention a person, a committee, a body or a company, for instance? It would be nice to know'. Several clients had to obtain an article to see whether or not it was relevant to their interests. This happened at Harwell as well as Trent, and 60 per cent of readers there indicated that titles were insufficiently informative on their own. From 20 per cent to 50 per cent of items requested turn out to be not what the title suggested. However clients are afraid that if more is added about each item, there will be more bulletin to read!

*Reading load*. A client at Harwell said that his ideal bulletin would be two pages long. Length and problems of receiving bulletins in batches because of discontinuities in the production system were the main problems experienced under this heading. If reading the bulletin represented too much of a task, it might not get read at all.

### Outcome of the evaluations

At Trent, as a result of reading the report on the news bulletin, the librarian has put in hand some changes. More 'serious' titles are to be scanned for the bulletin. Each bulletin item is to be recorded once, under the most appropriate heading, a clear separation of subject heading, title and added keywords is to be made, and more descriptive comment is to be added to some items. A list of the 100 most used subject headings is to be given in the bulletin. The librarian's report to the director presented the cost and value information obtained in the survey. The outcome was that the director was satisfied that some staff were benefiting from *Education News*, and more important, that the librarian knew what he was doing. There is no indication of how the survey has affected the much more complex situation at Harwell.

# References

Blick, A. R., Magrill, D. S., 'The value of a weekly in-house current awareness bulletin serving pharmaceutical research scientists', *Information Scientist*, March 1975, 19–28.

Flowerdew, A. D. J., Whitehead, C. E. M., 'Cost-effectiveness and cost/benefit analysis in information science', OSTI Report 5206, October 1974, 20–7.

Martyn, J., 'Library and information services provided to local government officials and others in Leicestershire: a study of costs and benefits', *Aslib Proceedings*, 1980.

Morley, R. A., Hopkins, J., 'Current awareness service for social scientists', in *Project for evaluating the benefits from university libraries: final report*, ed. J. Hawgood, R. A. Morley, University of Durham 1969, Chapter 7, OSTI Report 5056.

Nightingale, R. A., 'A cost-benefit study of a manually-produced current awareness bulletin', *Aslib Proceedings*, April 1973, 153–7.

Orr, R. H., 'The scientist as an information processor', in *Communication among scientists and engineers*, ed. C. E. Nelson and D. K. Pollock, Heath, Lexington 1970, 143–89.

Whitehall, T., 'Cost, value and effectiveness of library and information services', M.Phil thesis, Loughborough University of Technology, April 1984.

Whitehall, T., 'Current awareness in education: an evaluation of Trent Polytechnic's *Education News*', *Aslib Proceedings*, September 1985, 355–70.

# Index

Abstracting 11, 49
Abstracting services
   as a source of items for CAS 7-9,
     37
Abstracts
   availability of 11, 17
ACOMPLINE database 67
Address labels for bulletins 31, 54,
   59-60
Adlib computer package 48, 54, 59,
   61-2, 63, 68
Administration
   of co-operative information bulletin
     32
Alternative cost
   as a measure of value 97-8
Anthony, J.L. 75
Arnold, D.V. 77
*Atlas Biomedical Condensates* 37-8
Atomic Energy Research Establishment, Culham 75
Atomic Energy Research Establishment, Harwell
   databases produced from primary
     literature scanning 79, 83
   information bulletin 83, 91
     cost of 94
     effectiveness of 101-2
     value of 97-100
   local computer network 78
   on-line bulletin 79
   use of manual and computer SDI
     together 77
   use of primary and secondary
     sources in CAS 83

Beechams Pharmaceuticals 82, 84
Benefit from current awareness service
   3, 74, 85-6
   measuring 91-100
Bibliographic databases
   as a source of items for CAS 7-9,
     37
Blick, A.R. 77, 82, 92
Bought-in macroprofiles 5-6, 16
Bought-in SDI 9, 16
British Gas 81
British Steel Corporation 79, 80, 82
Bulletins, current awareness
   appearance of 11-12

arrangement of 2, 12, 93
bought-in from outside 4-6, 81
centralised vs. decentralised 25-7
compilation online 56-8, 60
compilation from a commercial
   database 34-47
of contents pages 4, 5
costs of 6, 91-103
effectiveness of 11-12, 101-3
frequency 93
on-line 12, 78, 79-80
production of
   co-operative 27-33
   use of computers in 34-47,
     54-69, 78-9, 80
size 2, 11, 53, 93, 102
value of 6, 99-100
*see also Daily Intelligence Bulletin*
Bush Boake Allen, Ltd 82

CAS *see* Current awareness services
Clerical work
   reduction by computerisation 61-3
Clients of current awareness services
   benefits for 3, 6-7, 74
   and co-operative bulletins
     requirements of 30-31
   cost to 6, 92, 102
   interests of 9-11
   and co-operative bulletins 28-9
   at Trent and Harwell
     interviews with 94-100
Collison, R.L. 11
Commercial databases *see* Databases
Computer production
   of co-operative information
     bulletins 32
   of current awareness bulletins 42,
     60, 61-2, 69, 78-9
     cost 68
     use of external database in 7-9,
       34, 47
     work involved 61-2, 67, 68
   of current awareness services ix,
     75-80
   of the *Daily Intelligence Bulletin*
     60-9
   of database as well as bulletin 63-7
   and industrial information units
     78-80

106